SELL Without Selling Your SOUL

How Smart Women
Connect, Communicate,
And Close With Confidence

by Liz Wendling

Women & Co Press
Littleton, CO

SELL Without Selling Your SOUL

ISBN: 978-098-467-6675

Website: www.lizwendling.com
E-mail: liz@lizwendling.com

Printed in U.S.A.
Published by Women & Co Press
4385 South Balsam Street
Suite 11-201
Littleton, CO 80123

First Edition

Edited by Paulette K. Kinnes
Cover and interior design by Maryann Brown Sperry

Dedication

Dedicated to my fun and loving family.
You are the most significant and divine people in my life.
I am blessed to have the support, love, and laughter
that you bring to my existence.

Acknowledgements

To Paulette K. Kinnes, my editor and now a forever friend. Thank you for the many phone calls and countless hours that you have put into my passion and for steering me through the book writing process with such grace.

Table Of Contents

Introduction

If you have a business, you are in sales. Sales is the only way to keep your business in business. There is no other way to stay in business besides someone hiring you and paying you for what you do. Really, not one!

Every woman has the ability to a sell without selling her soul! Let's get crystal clear on my definition of what selling is and what it is not. Selling is NOT about being pushy, salesy, or aggressive. It is NOT about force, manipulation, or putting people in a headlock until they hire you. It is NOT about annoying and harassing people until they say yes to you or take out a restraining order against you. Selling is the ability to develop strong, trusting relationships with people. Selling is about stepping into your sales conversations with authenticity, competence, and rock solid confidence and doing it in a way that fits you and your personality. You choose how you want to sell.

Have you ever wondered how some women make selling look effortless? It's easy to assume that they have a natural talent for sales. Maybe you think that some women were born with inherent sales talent. Not so. They make selling and closing business look easy because they have been capably trained. These women took the time to learn how to sell in a way in which potential clients are drawn to them. They recognized that the fastest way to produce a transformation in their business bottom line was to acquire the skill that enabled them to successfully motivate and guide today's new consumer to move from a potential client to a paying client. They became sales magnets. They attract because of who they are and how they authentically interact with others.

Women have been telling me for years that they have been yearning to find a way to sell that's right for them, that feels authentic, and that is gratifying to execute on a consistent basis. That is why I wrote *Sell Without Selling Your Soul.*

Once you understand that there is a better way and a new approach, your selling skills will improve immediately. You'll find that you can use these strategies and sell yourself in almost any situation. You get to bury the sales tricks, gimmicks, and out-of-date techniques that no longer work.

This book is for all female entrepreneurs, women business owners, and salespeople. It's for professionals who play a vital role in marketing, selling, and running a thriving business. It's for every woman who knows that the achievement level of her business and her income is dependent on the ability to sell herself first and everything else second.

Selling is about human relationships. Whether online or offline, selling is about people, and it always will be. The better your ability to connect and communicate with another human being, the more business you will win. No doubt that technology will continue to change and enhance some of the routine activities used in selling, but the one thing that can't be replaced is the human element. Only so much of the selling process can be outsourced to a computer.

In this fiercely competitive economy, every meeting, every sales call, and every interaction with a potential customer is critical to the survival of your business. Now is your time to learn how to sell in a way that allows you to keep your soul intact and utilize a selling approach that aligns with your values and integrity.

Few professionals will have the power, the patience, or the persistence to do the work that must be done to master the sales and client conversion process. You do. Step onto the field. This liberating and exhilarating sales and client conversion game is real, and it produces champions. Will you be one of them?

I encourage you to read this book in its entirety. You may think that it makes sense to scan the book, skip over paragraphs, and speed-read through the chapters that you need the most, but that approach will be futile. You may even think, *Her ideas won't work in my business. Been there, done that, and I failed. My business is different. I already tried that, and it flopped.*

Please consider two things: your willingness to suspend any disbelief that these concepts won't work and your willingness to work on the concepts detailed on the remaining pages. Begin by forming your own self-fulfilling prophecy that you can do it. Stop looking for what won't work and start paying attention to what can.

I am not suggesting that you integrate all of the ideas at once. I hope that you implement them at a pace that is realistic for you. Try one of the ideas. Get proficient at it. Then try another and then another. Continue until your skills evolve to a higher level of performance.

It is up to you to internalize and find what works for you and then incorporate those habits into your daily activities, thus becoming more at ease with them over time.

My intention is to interrupt old mindset patterns and disrupt antiquated sales habits that don't serve you anymore.

Disclaimer: You can continue to sell the way you always have. You can engage clients the same way that you've been doing. This is fine if you're willing to accept the same results. But you will have to meet with four times as many people, you will work twice as hard, and you will deal with more rejection than any human being should have to endure. Or you can build a strong framework, create key steps, and use modern sales methodologies to win more business.

Throughout the book, and to avoid repetition, you will notice that I use terms like consumer, clients, potential clients, prospects, buyers, and customers interchangeably. I also use descriptors related to sales, conversion, converting clients, closing business, sealing the deal, and selling skills to mean the same thing.

Also, you may notice several words describing business owners, such as professionals, specialists, experts, gurus, and authorities.

Let's begin the journey into the stimulating and lucrative world of selling!

Thank you for having trust and faith in me and for believing that selling without selling your soul is possible. It is time to leave your old way of doing business behind and move into evolved ways of closing business and converting clients.

I invite you to play full-out, to bring your A-game, to give it your all, and to be ready to invest 100 percent of yourself. I look forward to our paths crossing someday soon and to hearing the incredible stories of your accomplishments. The approach outlined in this book has worked for me and thousands of other women. And it can work for you too.

May your growing pains be minimal and your transformation exceptional. Know that my heart and passion are on every page.

Let's do it!

Chapter 1

Business As Usual Is Over

It is almost impossible not to have noticed the transformation that is occurring in the business landscape. You don't have to look far to find proof that plenty of things are not working like they used to when it comes to attracting clients and closing business. So, if ever there was a time for new, it is now! Times have changed, and business as usual has gone the way of the dinosaur. The consumer, the economy, and the business environment have altered forever, and they continue to evolve so fast that even the smartest women business owners and professionals have trouble keeping up. The journey to business growth and personal greatness isn't a fixed point at which you arrive and stay forever. Everything changes, and so must you.

The landscape has become more competitive and more technology-oriented than ever before. Consumers have a gazillion more choices than even a few years ago. Competition is at an all-time high, and you are competing with millions of others for clients and business. These days just showing up, having a stellar product or service, being awesome at what you do, and delivering superior service is no longer enough to guarantee a substantial income. What does guarantee additional income is knowing what it takes to motivate the consumer to take action with you, not your competition.

Being a rock star at sales and client conversion is not reserved for ultra-talented, highly-motivated, and magnetically-charismatic women. With a precise skill set and a healthy mindset, every woman can be extraordinary at converting leads into clients and closing sales and do it with authentic confidence.

Sales and client conversion are the lifeblood of your business. Without clients you will not have a business. It all boils down to using a clear-cut, updated, and repeatable system that is customized for you and your business and that transports you to your intended destination.

The women I know invested in enhancing their sales skills. They knew that modern skills would translate to higher income today, tomorrow, and well into the future.

Are you open to looking under the hood of your existing business and mindset as they relate to selling? Are you willing to learn some new skills and unlearn others? Are you eager to master how to relate, connect, and communicate with discerning consumers? Are you prepared to take the skills and abilities that you already have and adjust and modernize them so that you may achieve your intended results more effectively? I anticipate that your answer is not only yes but *hell, yes!*

The women who excel in this business climate are those who recognize that previous methods of sales won't work like they used to. The entire process needs an overhaul, and some elements of it need a full-on burial. What you've been taught has become obsolete and becomes more irrelevant with each passing year.

The traditional model of selling is too limiting and inadequate for today's sophisticated and experienced consumer. The old-school modes of the past have been replaced with more progressive and innovative strategies that consumers not only appreciate, they also notice. Since the rest of the world is evolving in reaction to consumers becoming more well-informed and Internet-savvy, it is in your best interests to evolve as well, or you will face extinction.

I know that you already know how to get the phone to ring and that you are scheduling daily or weekly client consultations. You are doing your homework, and you research a potential client or company. You are networking, doing a bit of marketing, using social media, and your business is in motion, but you aspire to close more business and convert more clients. You want to discover what works and rid yourself of what doesn't when it comes to sales. You are a driven and serious female professional who is no longer willing to stand still and remain where you are.

Almost every professional must speak on the phone or meet face-to-face with potential clients. These experts have one thing in common. They all need stellar sales and communication abilities and contemporary conversion skills. I have listed more than a dozen of these kinds of professionals for you here: accountant, architect, attorney, engineer, investment banker, caterer, chiropractor, coach, consultant, dentist, editor, graphic artist, landscaper, interior decorator, insurance agent, mortgage lender, nutritionist, photographer, real estate broker, website designer.

All of the powerhouse women who have revised and revamped their skills are flourishing and will tell you that a massive payoff is headed your way when you make a few modifications and that a fortune is at stake if you don't. Have you tallied up the money that you are leaving on the table? If not, let's take a look at it and do some math.

Use your own business, and pretend that an average client means an additional $2,000 to your business. Imagine that two additional clients per month choose you instead of your competition. This will net you an additional $4,000 per month, or $48,000 per year.

This increased income would not involve any extra advertising or marketing costs. You would still have the same number of meetings and consultations, but more people would hire you because you are different than the other professionals with whom these prospects meet.

You restructured your approach and sales and consultation language so that you didn't resemble or sound like the competition. Plus, you ensured that your entire process was more streamlined and effective. You put forth the same amount of energy with a much different result.

Can you live with the kind of loss outlined above? If that number makes you gasp, stay with me.

Will this process be easy? Nope! Nothing is easy or painless on the journey to business bliss. If building an empire was easy, wouldn't everyone have a booming business and a whopping bank account? I'm pretty certain that if victory was a piece of cake, word would have gotten around. Anything worth doing and doing well takes time and energy. The hardest part is creating energy and momentum and keeping it going. It's igniting the fire first and then every once in a while throwing another log on that fire to keep it burning. Once you start, it becomes easier, and soon you'll be leaving your competition in the dust.

Unpleasant News Alert: If you're seeking a shortcut or a silver bullet to prosperity, it's not on the pages of this book. If you're looking for a book that is going to tell you exactly what to say in every situation, that's not here either. That would do more harm than good. There are no words that work in every conversation or selling situation.

No step-by-step recipe or one-size-fits-all sales and client consultation formula exists that will guarantee success. Such a guarantee is not practical, nor would it be honest. Every prospect, every conversation, and every industry is different and requires adaptation and adjustment to those differences. There is no black and white. Each situation is as unique as the people involved in it.

Rather, this book is about change. It is about preparing you to acquire a fresh set of skills and concepts that will enable you to break through the limitations of the ancient model of sales. Out with the old, in with the new, as they say.

I will offer you a few examples, but I am not going to give you scripts for every possible scenario. Nor will the examples I do offer be applicable for every person, industry, service, or product. Providing you a word-for-word script for every potential situation would wind up being the lengthiest book ever authored. You know your industry, and you will need to be imaginative and modify the language to fit your individual needs.

Many professionals have asked me to hand them a script that they can use day in and day out that would compel someone to hire them. They think that to convert more clients and close more business all they need is a sheet of paper with a script on it. Scripts aren't natural. They diminish your power and interfere with your ability to be inquisitive and present in a client conversation.

There is nothing wrong with scripting out your own language. By all means, write things down so you remember the stages and steps. Scripted language is effective if you leave room to inject your personality, style, and flair into it.

I tell people that super scripting causes selling blind spots and missed sales opportunities. I explain that placing too much reliance on a script, when the client zigs or zags or changes the direction of your verbal exchange, you won't know how to reply because you're not prepared. You will have an, *Oh shit, that's not on my script* moment.

Celebrated actors know their lines and know where they are in their scenes. However, some are known for going off-script because something needs to be interjected in that moment, and this allows for the enchantment that happens on stage. You have full permission to do the same. Go ahead and be focused and on task, but leave room for spontaneity.

When you construct your own language, in your style and with your personality, it sounds genuine, and you will use it. I will always help people design their consultation language and assist them in coming close to what they should say, but giving someone a word-for-word script is unworkable and inefficient.

Let your competition sound salesy, phony, and scripted while you knock someone's socks off with your dazzling ability to converse in a more authentic way.

> My favorite quote, which hangs in my office, reads:
> *What holds so many people back is an unwillingness to pay the price, to make the effort to sacrifice their ease and comfort.* ~ Orison Marden

It's tempting to follow the masses, to get sucked into believing that there is a uncomplicated route to abundance. The truth is, no quick fix exists. It's all about you and how much you are willing to invest to get to where you want to go.

Picture yourself watching late-night TV infomercials that promise you thinner thighs, sculpted arms, and a flatter stomach in just minutes a day with an easy-to-use contraption. Imagine a pill that melts away pounds of fat without you having to diet or exercise and that allows you to eat nothing but your favorite high-carbohydrate foods. This would be pure nonsense mixed with a ton of B.S. and a healthy dose of hype.

It is human nature to seek the easy way out. It is disappointing to observe how some people today look to hop on the fastest train on which they find the least discomfort. I call it the *You-mean-I-have-to-work-at-this* syndrome. Every day women let opportunities fall through the cracks and leave money on the table because they choose easy over efficient. Loads of people prefer the quick-fix over a long-lasting solution.

Some allege that *easy* is the ultimate advertising hook of all time. The lure of laziness is widespread. Numerous companies and industries make extreme claims that achievement in business takes almost no effort. You are too intelligent to fall for that garbage. Believing that nonsense sends you right back to the beginning to start all over again.

You won't be able to revamp your business overnight, but you will be able to transform it over time by taking the key steps that ensures its success.

Awaken from the delusion that somehow you are going to be able to make selling and client conversion painless and uncomplicated, and face the truth that you will have to lean in, do the work and participate in the process.

For the best sales results, you must make adjustments and take instant and deliberate action until you produce the outcomes that you want. Otherwise, you will have to settle for sales scraps.

I know it seems obvious that action is essential. Taking action is the only trajectory to profits. Despite the simplicity of this concept, there is a perpetual shortage of people who excel at accomplishing their desired goals. The habit of launching ideas into action is a prerequisite to getting things done.

The action that I'm talking about isn't trying something for a week or a month and declaring, *that didn't work. I tried everything. Nothing that I am doing is generating results. I'm not cut out for this business owner thing.*

I talk to professionals every day who spend enormous amounts of time talking and thinking about taking action. What a colossal waste of time and energy. You can think about losing twenty pounds all day long, but if you don't get your ass moving, nothing will happen. Thinking about exercising will not make you physically fit. Knowing is not the equivalent of doing. Most people over-know and under-do. Knowledge doesn't produce results, action does. The best results come from action and mastery of certain skills.

Jim Rohn professed, *You can't hire someone else to do your push-ups for you. You must do them yourself if you are to get any value out of them.*

Chapter 2

Your Selling Methods Must Evolve With The Times

If you are like a legion of women business owners, entrepreneurs, and sales professionals, you are probably responsible for most or all of the selling for your business. Some of you may be selling with little or no formal sales training, and you are not yielding the results you desire. Perhaps you've accumulated a number of sales methods from training classes or books but have not yet found your groove and the best way to fit them into your business puzzle.

On top of that you may still be using a sales approach and selling techniques that were invented three decades ago. You're using sales strategies, words, and phrases that come out of the dusty sales books of yesteryear. And you may even sound like everyone else in your industry. There was a time, decades ago when old-school sales techniques worked. They were developed at a different time, in a different economy and a different world where the internet didn't exist. It is time to kick up your heels and update your outdated sales and conversion strategies.

The sales and business communication process is more complex than ever, and many techniques are now ineffective and no longer in vogue. A different way of doing business has arrived and is here to stay. Are you ready to fully participate, or are you willing to wave to the world as it leaves you behind?

With the buying process now in the hands of the consumer, some business owners are not converting the number of clients they once did. To combat this problem, you must be ready to learn the cutting-edge sales skills that impress today's wise consumer.

The main challenge that you may face is not the mastering of the latest sales concepts, but rather transforming your current behavior and mindset. Why? Most human beings hate change. No one leaps into the arms of change. Change is difficult for most people, for you and your potential clients.

It has been stated that the only people who truly enjoy change, who embrace change and even cry out for it, are babies with a dirty diaper. Everyone else, not so much.

Change is not an innovative concept. Change didn't emerge in the 21st century to make your life and business miserable. Too often people whine, complain, moan, and protest this *change* thing and then wonder why their business is stalled. Change is not the problem. The real problem occurs when people are reluctant to let go, to lean in and accept it. You can either embrace change or hang out in the expensive place called the status quo, which goes hand-in-hand with mediocrity.

Consumers nowadays want a change, and they yearn for a variation in the sales relationship. Today's buyer is more sensitive to traditional sales techniques and is looking for someone to step out of the typical sales role and cultivate a different kind of relationship that is supportive and collaborative. She wants to work with someone who understands her concerns and assists her in the decision-making process.

The buyer has more choices and, therefore, can be more selective about where he takes his business. In other words, he no longer has to put up with the sales crap that was used on him in the past.

Selling has evolved because the consumer has evolved. You are meeting with clients who have less time, less money, and shorter attention spans than ever before. Today's consumer is more sophisticated, informed, in control, and skeptical. She is cautious of staged presentations and artificial pitches. Today's buyer is more value conscious, and she requires open, refreshing, honest, direct human communication from a trusted professional with whom she can build a long-term relationship. People don't have time for the B.S. anymore.

I wrote *Sell Without Selling Your Soul* to shorten your learning curve and help you dodge the pain and suffering that scores of professionals experience in the process of building their businesses. I am certain that you have noticed that what worked quite well for you five to seven short years ago is now antiquated. Possessing present-day consultation and selling skills will make an enormous difference in your business and propel you from having average client consultations to having exceptional client consultations.

Shifting to a new mindset and skill set takes time. Think of it like a crock pot, not a microwave. Slow and steady wins the race.

For most of us, the ability to sell is not as much intrinsic as it is a learned skill. I studied it too. It came more naturally to me, but I still needed coaching. I tried different methods, took sales classes, and practiced a lot. I had to win some and lose some. At one point, I was losing so many sales that it was destroying my self-confidence.

The problem was that I had no one to turn to and couldn't figure out what I was doing wrong. No sales coaches or consultants existed thirty years ago. I could not Google my issues and challenges. No mastermind groups, Facebooks groups, or online programs existed in which I could participate. I was on my own to figure it out.

I read books, and I attended training programs, but most of them didn't fit my needs. They all talked about control and manipulation. If that's what selling was, what did that make me? I felt like I was selling my soul to get the sale. I didn't want any part of it. I knew that there had to be a better way.

My sales managers encouraged me to make more calls, see more people, pick up the phone, hang in there, don't feel discouraged, change my attitude, don't take no for an answer. They were good at doling out motivational advice and giving me pep talks, but none of them offered me tools to help me improve. Pep rally-type meetings didn't help me close more sales or help me to figure out what I was doing wrong.

Back then, sales was an industry dominated by men, with lots of old-school techniques and hard sales tactics. I was met with daily rejection. I heard *No* a lot. I heard, *Let me think about it. Call me in a few weeks. I need to check with my spouse.*

I knew that it wasn't the customer, the economy, the territory, my boss, my age, my gender, or the product that I was selling. The one thing holding me back from the dreams that I had was me and my sales communication skills and my confidence. I set out on an expedition to become more comfortable in sales. I changed my language and changed my results.

I began talking to people like they were a family member and someone I cared about. It made a remarkable difference in my ability to connect and engage with complete strangers. I analyzed what I was doing that was causing people to become more attracted to me and my offering. I noted that when I spoke to people from my heart, not my head, I made better connections. I met more clients, closed more sales, gained more referrals, and had so much more fun.

Once the skills and the sales language became a part of my confident self, I never stopped. I connected with people, communicated in a way that was authentic, and I closed with confidence. I have modified my process, and refined it, over the last three decades, and it's what I teach in workshops, seminars, and to my private coaching clients.

I'm a cut-to-the-chase, straight-talking Jersey gal with a gift for streamlining complex concepts. I teach people real-world strategies that may be implemented right away. I don't teach a plethora of redundant and stale sales techniques straight out of the 1980s. I teach the meat, the nuts and bolts, and the concrete ideas for selling in today's marketplace.

You are likely reading this book because your sales results and closing rates are not where you want them to be, and you have a desire to change that. Perhaps you are already good at client conversion but want to move up a notch to rock star status. The fact that you are engaged and discovering this process is a clear indication that you are ready to step up to play a better game.

One of the most exciting things about sales and client conversion is that you are in full control of what does and does not happen in your business. Your income, your free time, your family's quality of life, the fulfillment of your values, and the achievement of your dreams are up to you. You call the shots. You control your money making capabilities. You set your standards. I have never seen a professional fail because she set her standards too high.

Warning: You may deny that some of my ideas, concepts, and tools will work. Know that when you feel the most resistance, that is the message that you need to hear the most, and this is when you know that a change needs to be made. If an idea rubs you the wrong way, I encourage you to confront that idea. You may need to hear it. Resistance is nature's way of telling you to pay attention, take notice, and listen up because there is a lesson or skill to be learned.

Don't oppose the changes because they're inconvenient and awkward at the moment. Resistance only makes the process arduous and more excruciating. Be willing to look at new opportunities with an objective mind so that you may build a thriving business!

The rewards that you reap will be the direct result of what you sow in your endeavors. Like any other undertaking in life, the bulk of the responsibility lies with you.

Chapter 3

The Power Of The Process

Devising an engaging client experience is not a matter of luck, hope or rolling the dice, rather it involves your capacity to conduct a focused sales conversation and connect and communicate in such a way that potential clients perceive your value within the first few moments of meeting you. You jump into the lead and become the front-runner.

Your selling process for engaging with prospects is the perfect opportunity for differentiation. Every interaction is a chance to stand out and offer your prospects a different experience than your competition does. You create your WOW factor.

When your client meetings fall into a predictable pattern and expected structure, you will not differentiate yourself, and you will not garner attention. Using an all-purpose approach feels insincere, artificial, and anticipated. It is boring and ho-hum as well.

Every professional uses a process, day after day, consciously and unconsciously. In sales, your success, or lack of results, is always obvious. Either you succeed in bringing in business and hitting your revenue goals or you don't. Only you know if your process is working for you. Only you know if it is draining you or fulfilling you.

If you Googled the words *sales* or *lead* or *client conversion process*, you would collide with more than nine million results. From those results, a dizzying array of concepts, systems, procedures, and approaches would hit you between the eyes.

Your task is to harmonize your consultation process with your prospective client's buying process. We all have a process that we use to help us make decisions. Buying decisions vary from person to person. Some people make rapid decisions, others ponder and deliberate forever before they come to a decision.

I make swift decisions, seldom change my mind, and do not suffer from buyer's remorse. I know what I want, and if it feels right, I buy. Others contemplate, meditate, and ruminate about whether to commit to a yes or no. Some research for weeks or months. Some will never make a decision. To them, making no decision is a decision made.

The sales process is unique to every professional. A pastry chef has a process for baking a pie, a Super Bowl quarterback has a process for throwing the football, an artist has a process for painting a picture, and you must have a process for constructing an incredible client interaction. Anyone who is prosperous has an identifiable process behind that prosperity.

A structured process takes the pressure off of you and places the primary focus on your client. Freedom lives in structure. Structure frees you up to be more present, connected, spontaneous, natural, and more human.

When you have a process, you can relax, be unflappable. Rather than focusing on yourself and worrying about screwing up, you are now at ease and engrossed in one thing—your prospective client.

A process delivers predictable and reliable results. When a process is effective, you know why it works. When you can predict a result, you will be thrilled to repeat it over and over, which will generate more closed business.

Every time I lead a workshop or training, a few people emphatically decline to use a structured process. They flat-out refuse to follow a step-by-step approach that produces results. They fold their arms, stomp their feet, and throw a grown-up tantrum. They do this because they would rather think that they are right and stay stuck where they are than make money and win more business. They would rather go with the flow, take a chance, and hope that the sale is consummated.

The people who don't use a defined sales process use the ineffective *winging it* process. Their process is not structured or logical, it's scattered and inefficient and produces poor results. Professionals who use the *winging it* process utter things like, *No one is buying right now. Everyone tells me they'll think about it, but I never hear back from them. People don't have any money right now. No one ever returns my calls. I can't get anyone to say yes.* Hmmm, I wonder why?

The word process comes from the Latin word procedure, which means to proceed, and is a series of operations or stages that lead to a specific outcome. The textbook definition of a sales or conversion process is: a structured, systematic, logical, and documented step-by-step approach to selling a product or service in which a progression of defined steps is followed and results in the completion of a sale.

My modified definition of a conversion process is: a set of structured and defined steps that move an interested client into an invested client and a raving fan. It is a process that flows and is flexible, it is not rigid and formal.

Don't underestimate the vitality hidden in this tool until you fully understand the impact that it will have on your business or practice. A sales process is a must-have in your business toolbox.

If the sales process is the roadmap to success that facilitates salespeople to close more sales in a shorter period of time, then salespeople should clamor to use this tool.

Droves of individuals would rather go with the flow and take a chance that they will be able to close the business. Some have two or three skills in their arsenal and get lucky now and then.

Mastering one or two skills alone won't produce the same results as grasping and mastering the entire process. There are parts and pieces to every process, and some of them are distinctive for every industry. But the capacity of this tool is not fully realized until you use all of the parts and pieces together. Applying the principles of the entire process leaves nothing to chance.

Every sale is the result of a series of consistent behaviors and actions. There are an abundance moving parts to the process: building chemistry and making a connection, inspiring trust, creating value, asking insightful questions, discussing what you offer, talking about fees and budgets, handling objections, securing the business, disclosing how you will communicate moving forward, and concluding the sale.

One size does not fit all. There are various other nuances to every process. It is up to you to build your own process. You need a custom process to ensure potency and efficiency in your business. Designing processes is one of my favorite things to do for clients because the return on their investment is so monumental.

Chapter 4

Are You Updated Or Outdated?

A number of professionals are shocked to find out that they are saying and doing things on a regular basis in their initial sales conversations and consultations that out of sync and clash with how human beings are wired to buy and be influenced. Many are using a *hand-me-down* sales approach that their boss, or co-worker taught them ten years ago, some are doing what they learned from a sales book, and some are doing and saying what others in their industry are doing. Their traditional and standardized approach is so ingrained in them that they don't realize that it is old-school and no longer effective.

Most people believe that they have a solid understanding of the consumer buying process. Business owners are convinced that when they sit down to meet with a prospect, they have all the skills they need to transform that prospect into a paying client. The reality is that a number of people are using outdated techniques and communication skills that are no longer applicable with today's Internet-empowered consumer.

If I queried a hundred professionals as to whether they are interacting with the consumer using an evolved approach, 95 percent of them would say that they are. But it is this very self-deception that is causing them to be the runner-up. Coming in second place is pricey.

By the time the consumer meets you face-to-face or talks to you on the phone, a whopping 65 to 70 percent of their decision-making activity is complete. They are doing their homework and educating themselves. You can be assured that your prospective clients will bounce from website to website to research you, Google you, read about your credentials and expertise, and check out your ratings and reviews. Isn't that what we all do?

The remaining 25 to 30 percent of their journey comes down to you. Will you engage, connect, and communicate with prospects in such a way that they do not need to visit the competition or resume shopping? Will your one-on-one communication skills and approach be current, or will it look like you got stuck in the 1970s? Will you be an evolved professional, or will you lose business to one?

The initial consultation is that make-or-break meeting that will determine whether someone will hire you on the spot or hire your competition. Since new clients are the lifeblood of every business, why not do all that you can to construct the most positive outcome and show up in a way that makes you stand out?

Now hear this. Sales and client conversion is not marketing. Often professionals think that they can market their way to a flourishing business. They believe that they can invest in marketing and that that exposure will be enough to convert clients. Never!

All the marketing in the world will not yield results if you don't know how to convert a lead into a paying client. Your marketing speaks to the masses. Your sales and lead conversion process takes place on a one-to-one basis. You still must be able to conduct persuasive conversations that move, inspire, and motivate people to hire you. No one pulls out their credit card or checkbook because you know how to market. Exposure is important, but the ability to engage potential clients and close the business is the only way to stay in business. Marketing opens the door, and your conversion skills close the sale.

Sales and conversion skills are the most overlooked skills by numerous business owners, but they pack the potential to be the most lucrative of all.

Sales and conversion skills tend to be the last skills in which professionals invest. They instead choose to invest in a beautiful website, shoot videos and build a robust social media presence. They take classes, go to events, network, meet prospects for coffee, attend conferences, spend hours at luncheons, and everything else under the sun. Then when all of their efforts start to work and someone wants to find out more about their product or service, they are not prepared to make the most out of the opportunities that present themselves. All of their hard work is not maximized because they lack the potent skills necessary to inspire someone to buy.

Prospective clients arrive, wanting to talk to specialists to find out more about what they do, and then those specialists blow it and step into *winging it* mode. They conduct half-assed consultations with negligible structure and no value. Or they attempt to sell too early in the conversation. The meeting ends with, *Thanks for your information. I am going to think about it. I have no money. I can't afford it. Call me in a few weeks.*

Don't make the mistake of an amateur and disregard certain steps or skip steps in your process in an attempt to speed things up. While you may meet with a favorable outcome in the short run, in the long run this is not a sustainable strategy.

In time, as you foster your own style and approach, you will develop an intuition for when some flexibility is required, based on specific situations.

When I am role-playing during my workshops and consultations, I often observe a professional jump to a solution too soon. In the rush to sell something, business owners bypass the part of the process where they ask questions and dig deep into the prospects issues and challenges. As soon as the potential client mentions a problem, they swoop in with their ideas about how to solve it. They miss the brilliance of asking questions that get to the root of the issue.

For example, a prospective client pronounces, *I'm struggling to come up with my language and a strong call to action on my marketing material. I know that we are missing something in our business messaging, but we are stumped as to what that is.* The professional sees this as an opportunity to sell, lean in, and hit the gas pedal and says, *Well, some of the best marketing minds in the business are here at my company. I can help you with that. We can review your language to see what is missing and help you find a powerful message.*

S-L-O-W your roll. Pump the brakes. Hold your horses. You are likely making premature judgments and impulsive assumptions, and in doing so you shut down and derail the conversation. You don't know enough about the prospect's situation or needs to propose the best solution. You are engaging in premature selling. And another sale, as well as income, flies out the window.

It's like telling your doctor that you injured your shoulder and that you have been in pain for six months. The doctor asks a question or two and replies, Why don't we get you scheduled for surgery right away so that the healing process may begin? We can repair the rotator cuff and clean some things up while we have you under anesthesia. How about next week?

You're thinking, Damn, that was fast. No additional questions? No x-rays? No physical therapy? No other alternatives? The doctor rushed to judgment and assumed that surgery was the right solution for the ache in your shoulder. That is not only selling too soon, it is also malpractice. Pay attention to how soon your rush to sell.

These days, potential clients don't want to make an appointment with you or schedule a call with you if they feel like you do and say the same thing as everyone else. They have changed the way they buy. In turn, you need to change the way you sell. Everyone that you talk to won't need what you are selling, just as everyone is not a candidate for shoulder surgery. Resist diagnosing or selling too fast.

Curb Your Enthusiasm

Just when I think an out-of-date sales technique has been buried for good, it rears its ugly head. In the traditional world of selling methods, you may have been taught that you must have a lot of energy and enthusiasm in your client engagements. You've been trained that you should show excitement about your product or service. You've been told that enthusiasm is contagious and that your positive emotions will be transmitted to the prospect. If you can engender the same passion in the prospect, they'll buy whatever you are selling. That is about as old-school and phony as it gets.

Nothing screams the 1970s quite like that advice. It's annoying and insincere. This garbage has been around for more than fifty years and is *still* being taught by some sales gurus, who have decided to forego updating their approach, have abstained from changing with the times, and who continue to teach archaic sales skills.

I'm not suggesting that you need not be enthused or energetic in your client consultations. But the discriminating consumer no longer responds to that type of pushy and phony hype. It triggers negative feelings and turns people off because that tactic has been used on people for decades.

Whether face-to-face or on the phone, your energy and enthusiasm should be considered and examined. It's nice to be eager about what you do and have a passion for what you sell, but that eagerness may overwhelm the prospect and cause her to be skeptical. If you talk too much or jump in too early to present your solutions, you look like you're more interested in the sale than in getting to know the client's needs.

Too much energy and springing right into your solution with a rehearsed sales pitch comes off as disingenuous and salesy. Of course, the flip side to this is low energy and no enthusiasm, where you give the conversation reins to your prospect and allow him to guide the meeting and drive the conversation. Neither one works.

You can't impart your energy and exhilaration to someone else unless you have a meaningful conversation that gets *them* enthused. They have to feel it for themselves. Appropriate gusto is an asset in the client conversation. Inappropriate zeal is a negative factor and always results in your prospect's walls going up, and her trust in you evaporates. Enthusiasm is no substitute for passion. When you're passionate about what you do, your enthusiasm will shine through in a natural but softer, less hard-hitting way.

Pro tip: When you meet someone face-to-face or on the phone, gauge his energy level. You do this by asking questions and letting the potential client do most of the talking. Watch or listen to how he answers your questions and responds to your energy. If you're witnessing smiles, nods, and verbal agreement, keep it up. If you're observing fidgets, wandering eyes, silence, or other signs of distress, tone it down. Be yourself, but watch the level of your intensity.

This is not an exact science. If you have a lot of enthusiasm, don't run away from it! But think about how you're expressing it. Use it as a way to demonstrate your passion for your work and your prospects.

Enthusiasm isn't a slick trick or sales technique. When it's genuine, it comes from your passion for what you sell and the value that you provide. It is contagious, and when mastered, it has enormous trust-building power. Find your own passion first, and genuine enthusiasm will follow.

Chapter 5

The Skills That Keep On Giving

If you gift yourself with the skills that keep on giving, you will never have to take the long, nauseating ride on the revenue roller coaster. These skills are sales skills.

Countless professionals have shared with me that they felt that selling and conversion skills were their greatest deficiency. When it came time to move into the initial consultation, they did not feel secure in their own skin. It wasn't that they didn't know what to say, it was that they couldn't deliver the information in a polished and professional way. They worried that they would sound pushy or come across as fake.

The result was that they never attempted to step into a selling role with authentic power and take charge of the process.

I don't mean taking charge by pulling out the sales hammer or bossing everyone around. I mean having the self-assurance to take the wheel and drive the conversation in the best direction for everyone involved.

Most people do what they're good at. You're probably tremendous at executing the services that you provide, and you enjoy your work. Most professionals are far better at showcasing their expertise and delivering on their services than they are at selling them. But in order to do the job that they enjoy, they must move into the sales role to attract clients and close sales with confidence.

When you have a plan, and you know how the conversion game is played, you triumph. No matter how clever you are, if you haven't had updated training and you don't know the rules, the odds of winning are stacked against you.

Just because you've flown on an airplane doesn't mean that you could jump in the cockpit of a 747 and lift the plane off the ground. You've had no formal training. The right knowledge and the right skills training equal exceptional results.

If you are like many specialists, you are nowhere near as confident and comfortable selling your products and services as you are delivering them. Some people turn their noses up at the thought of having to sell their expertise, so they never develop that skill. This damaging mindset makes their foundation weak and unstable and is the main reason why professionals don't generate the profits that they deserve.

Since we're all selling something, wouldn't it make sense to learn more about selling? Wouldn't it be better to remove the stigma associated with selling?

Before you can serve clients, you must influence them to hire you, and this starts with a well-functioning client conversion process.

If what you are doing right now was yielding the results that you require, you would already be where you want to be, wouldn't you? If your conversion strategies and sales attempts were enough to win you the clients that you need, you would have those clients. If the way that you sell right now was enough to close business, you would have no trouble building your business and increasing profits. If how you sell today isn't producing the results that you wish for, it is time to transform the way that you sell.

Despite the massive and obvious changes in the world, some experts still adhere to traditional business practices from decades ago. Clinging to the past will lead you to a certain dead end.

I'm not suggesting that you dump and destroy every sales method that you have ever used and start all over. But I am proposing that you scrutinize what you are doing now and see what might need a tweak, an overhaul, or a burial. Take a long, hard look at your current client conversion approach. Identifying, learning, and staying up-to-date with the right skills can turn a mediocre business into a major contender. It's not too late to make some adjustments and catch up to what some of your competitors are already doing and profiting from.

You already have an established routine and an acceptable way of conducting yourself when meeting new clients. Your routine has been adopted throughout your career, and it may be quite relaxed for you. You carry on your consultations without a lot of scrutiny related to what you say and how you conduct them. This routine is generating your current level of income. If you're reading this book, you are likely looking for the next level of prosperity. Let's find that level now!

Chapter 6

The New Savvier And Smarter Consumer

Welcome to the world that is controlled by today's self-educated consumer. For the first time in history the consumer is in control, and they know it. The Internet and social media have forever changed the way that people buy. Thanks to the power of technology and the ease of the Internet, with a few clicks of a mouse your ideal clients are bellying up to the all-you-can-read information buffet, devouring as much as they can about you and comparing you to your competition. This is happening on their terms, their time, and their turf, twenty-four hours a day, seven days a week.

Despite the massive and obvious changes in technology, communication, and innovation, some women in business are having a hard time letting go of the old and embracing the new. They are hanging on to dated strategies that cost them clients and opportunities.

In the past, consumers were limited, and their buying process was pretty straightforward. They had to contact you early in their decision-making process because you had the information they needed. Fast-forward to today, and buyers are gathering that information and educating themselves about their options. You are doing the same thing. This is the new normal.

Now consumers want and need an insightful, two-way dialogue, not a bunch of lip service and a universal approach. They don't want you to take them down a path of generic questioning or utilize a probing checklist that every other professional in your industry is using.

As an authority who is focused on providing results and value to those with whom you work, delving into the heart of what people truly want enables you to more accurately fulfill their needs.

Today's consumers crave something different, something better, something more meaningful, and something that not many people are willing to give them. They are screaming, *Be real with me. Help me solve my problems and challenges, show me that you can improve my situation. Help me see what I'm not seeing. Tailor your approach to me, ask me the type of questions that cause me to think in a different way. Challenge my current mindset, help guide me in my buying decision, and show me the value in what you offer. Please don't tell me things I already know, and don't just try to sell me. Don't insult my intelligence and waste my time. Put my needs first, or I will go to someone who will.*

And that someone is called your competition.

Consumers want you to have an intention that aligns with theirs and be a trusted resource. When you do this, you will look and feel different from every other expert with whom they visit. Your potential clients seek someone who cares, who understands, who can help them focus on the relevant information and discard all the rest. They need you to be prepared to work with them and guide them through the decision-making process. They would like you to be composed, confident, and ready for anything that comes your way.

A clever poker player wouldn't stroll into a casino, sit down at a table, wing it, and leave things to chance. Poker players know the value of the cards and the rules of the game.

They understand keen poker strategies, like knowing when to split a pair and when not to, knowing when to raise their bet, and knowing when to hold them or when to fold them. They read facial expressions and watch body language. They have an edge by knowing the odds and their competition. This is no different in business.

In the end, buyers want to know one ultimate thing, and that's whether you're going to take good care of them and do what you say you will do.

Your potential client doesn't care whether you are charming, witty, and have an outgoing personality. He doesn't care if you are calm, shy, or introverted. Whoever you are and whatever your demeanor, you must convey, not vocalize, a huge, bold, believable, and compelling promise: *I will take good care of you, I will do what I say I will do, and you are in good hands.*

I know what you are thinking. *I do that. I do make it all about the client. I don't pressure people. I am relaxed and show that I care and have the prospect's best interests in mind.* Maybe you do. But maybe you don't.

Some women say that they are heart-based, client-focused, or client-centric, but when the rubber meets the road there is little substance behind their words and intentions. There is no meat on the bone. You can proclaim all day long how you put your clients first and care about them, but if your potential client doesn't observe that in their interactions with you, you let them down and send them to do business with your competitor.

Words like, *I knew that sooner or later her true colors would shine through. She made a bunch of promises that she did not keep. He was another professional who said all the right things and then dropped the ball after he had my money and a signed contract in his hand.*

Countless people give themselves high grades on their ability to express genuine care and concern. It is far easier to declare that you do these things but trickier to execute them.

The best way to find out how well you're doing is to check your results. If you are not converting most of the people that you talk to, you may not be transmitting vibes and sending messages that indicate that you are different, and the prospect is picking up on that.

Buyers come to your meeting painting all professionals with the same brush. To them, all specialists are cut from the same cloth and should not be trusted. Make sure that you take the scissors out of the client's hand by acting in a manner that engenders instant trust.

No matter what you sell, you are also in the people business. People will come to you for your insight and expertise, your understanding, your ability to hear and see, and your ability to offer the best solution for their situation.

Have you ever noticed that in some sales training programs there is no trust training, no training to teach experts how to get over the major hurdle that is someone saying yes? Without breaking down the walls of trust it will be difficult, if not impossible, to close business. No trust equals no sale. We will cover that in a later chapter.

When people don't hire you on the spot or respond to your advice, they're telling you that they don't trust you enough to take action, yet. When people choose not to open up and be honest about their current situation, it's because they do not trust you enough to do so. When they reject your approach, they're telling you that they don't believe you. These clients are not telling you that you need to make better features and benefits presentations, handle their objections more in a more proficient manner, or be a smoother closer. They're telling you that they are not yet sold on you and your offer.

Of course, it's necessary to be good at what you do and to know your services or products, but few people have failed in business because they lacked product or service knowledge.

Many fail because they're not effective at building the high-trust client relationships that people yearn for these days. They are building surface trust, not deep and intentional trust.

The art of being deliberate, purposeful, ethical, and sincere when building trust will never become obsolete or passé. If you're not building high-trust client relationships on purpose, you are doing it by chance.

Listed below are ten insights into the mind of the new consumer and what they wish professionals would do. All ten are defined more in subsequent chapters.

1. **Skip the superficial small talk.** When meeting a potential client, specialists are taught to begin an initial meeting or consultation with small talk, to chat about the weather, traffic, parking, or commenting on what someone is wearing or a current event. *Did you have any trouble finding the building? Did you have any issues with parking? How was the traffic getting here? Is it hot enough out there?*

STOP! Enough already! Every other professional is using this thirty-year-old, antiquated approach. Contrived chit-chat does nothing to build rapport, create a strong connection, or make a dynamic first impression. Delete this old-school tactic from your repertoire immediately. Connect authentically, not artificially.

2. **Connect and relate to me.** People are looking for an authority who makes a sincere connection and who cares about them and their situation. They want you to take a genuine interest in them, give them your complete attention, and truly listen to them. When prospects don't feel a connection, they disconnect from you.

Disconnected people don't leap to hire you on the spot. They don't care if you can solve their problem. They don't care if you are the best in the business and come highly recommended. *The consumer thinks, I am hiring you as a person first and as a professional second. I am buying who you are and how you treat me, not just your expertise. Please make me feel like I matter and like I am not just another meeting or consultation.*

3. **Don't treat me like I am clueless about my options.** In the past, the traditional consultation approach relied on meeting

with a potential client willing to sit quietly and be educated, in a time when people had little knowledge and few choices. Professionals were taught not to sell but rather to educate. Don't sell yourself or your products or services. Educate, and the consumer will write you a check. Not anymore!

Treating prospects as if they don't know anything about your product or service is counterproductive, and you run the risk of alienating, aggravating, and upsetting them. Education is still important, but you need to educate people from where they are, not from where they used to be. Find out where a prospective client is regarding his knowledge and insight, and navigate the conversation from there. Strive to captivate, not educate!

4. **Help me see why you are different than your competitors.** The challenge that business owners have when attempting to communicate how they are different is that to potential clients they sound similar to their competition. When the consumer asks you how you are different or why she should retain your services, she doesn't want you to launch into a canned answer. *I have been a CPA for more than twenty-two years and have a stellar reputation in my industry. I am very proud of my practice and the superior service that I provide to all of my clients.*

Blah, blah, blah. The customer is thinking, *Tell me something that I can't find on your website. Give me something that I can't read in your bio.* You must articulate and connect the dots about why you are different and how that difference relates to her and her situation.

5. **I have a name, please use it.** A number of consumers asserted, *I was shocked that the professionals with whom I met never used my name in our entire conversation, except to greet me. I would never hire anyone who did not see me as a person with a name.*

How much is this negative habit costing you? How would you feel if your heart surgeon, financial planner, tax accountant, or interior designer never used your name in a consultation? Addressing your client by his name not only personalizes your conversation, it builds a deeper connection. Don't overdo it, though, that's creepy.

6. **Show me the value in your services, and I will care less about your fees.** Value is the difference between the fees you charge and the benefits that the prospective client perceives she will receive. Often the lack of perceived value makes clients shop on price. Your fees may be the only difference that clients may easily see and measure. You may be the best at what you do, but if you fail to sufficiently convey your value in a captivating and precise way, you will continue to lose to a professional who charges less than you do.

7. **Talk about me and my situation first.** In the first few moments of meeting you, the prospect does not care about you yet. Plenty of professionals drive ideal clients away by talking about themselves first. They feel obliged to demonstrate how clever and experienced they are by reciting facts about themselves. Encourage the client to speak first, and take the spotlight off of yourself. Promoting conversation on the part of the client does not mean asking, *What brings you in today? How may I help you?*

Those questions will likely irritate clients. First, you should know why they are there. Second, why ask the same banal, predictable questions?

I see women do this every day when I assess and observe initial meetings and conduct mock consultations. The consumer is thinking, *I don't care how long you've been in business or about all the other people you've helped. I care about myself, my issues, and solving my problems. You can talk about yourself later in the conversation, after you have showed me that you care about me.*

8. **Make the money conversation comfortable.** Acting weird when discussing your fees with a prospective client put doubts in his mind and raises suspicion. The consumer thinks, *If she is apprehensive discussing money, I know that I will be apprehensive about giving her any of my hard-earned money. Please tell me in plain and simple language what's involved.*

The prospect wants you to put her at ease by clarifying the rules of engagement and how money is collected. Look her in the eye, and don't choke or change your demeanor when discussing fees. She is watching.

9. **If you want my business, ask me for my business.** It is your job to ask for the business. Not asking for the business, especially if someone is a good prospect, is awkward. People don't always come out and state, *Sounds good, let's get started. Who do I make the check out to?* Asking for the business is like running to first base after hitting a line drive. It's expected. If you don't ask the question, especially if the prospect is a good fit, and make the move, you send a message to the client that you don't want or need his business or that you are uptight asking for it.

10. **Reinforce my intelligent decision to hire you.** When the consumer finally makes her decision and hires you, she wants you to say something that makes her feel like she made the right choice. Don't say, *Okay, let's get the paperwork started. Great, I am looking forward to working with you.*

Instead say, *Diane, thank you for trusting me to help you with your legal situation. Since your court date for your DUI is in two weeks, let's finalize some paperwork and talk about what we will need to get accomplished in the next twenty-four to forty-eight hours.*

These issues are not minor, they are major keys to genuinely influencing others. The more your approach is aligned with what the consumer wants, the more you stand out, pull yourself ahead of the pack, produce more referrals, and win more business.

Chapter 7

Everyone Sells Something, Including You

Given how essential sales is to the bottom line of every business, I am often shocked at how many people would rather have a root canal and a colonoscopy on the same day than embrace sales and discover how to be superior at selling. Each of us is blessed with different innate talents, skills, and gifts. For most, a proficiency for selling is not innate, it is a learned skill. Now is the time to eliminate all of the adverse feelings and negative beliefs about being a salesperson for your business so that you may tap into your true potential.

Multitudes of individuals carry a ton of unnecessary baggage related to the idea of sales and selling around with them. They tend to over-think and over-complicate what selling is. With love and compassion, I say drop your baggage, and get over it. Sales is like oxygen. You need sales to survive. Everyone sells something. If you don't agree with those statements, this chapter is going to painful to read. Since sales are how you get paid, please keep reading, nevertheless.

What stops women from generating more sales and building a thriving business are the things that they believe about why it is not possible or why it can't be done. Women make all kinds of excuses to not be the person responsible for sales and the person accountable to the bottom line.

Some women believe certain myths about selling that make it much more problematic for them to flourish. They deem selling sleazy, icky, immoral, and shady. They believe that they have to sell their soul to make a sale. As soon as they let go of these beliefs, their natural ability to communicate their value, from a place of integrity and genuineness, will materialize.

Another myth women believe about selling is that all they have to do is be authentic. Every day I hear people say that they want to be authentic in their sales and selling endeavors. Programs, podcasts, books, webinars, and two-day conferences devoted to teaching people how to sell authentically abound. Gurus suck people in by shouting and touting, *Follow me on the path to closing more sales by being yourself and selling with authenticity.*

Be authentic is a hyped-up way of saying be real, genuine, truthful, direct, honest, open, sincere. When did that become a unique approach? Isn't that what we are all supposed to do? Authenticity is not some innovative new business strategy. Being sincere is not a fresh and modern sales tactic. Being honest in the sales process is not a shocking concept. It is, however, a brilliant buzzword that makes professionals believe that all they need to do is show up, be nice, and be themselves, and they will have a booming business and a bulging bottom line.

Just be yourself and be authentic is damaging business advice because it only tells half of the success story. That business killing advice implies that no skills are necessary.

Of course, you need to be authentic in sales. You are supposed to be authentic in life as well. It is imperative that you sell from a genuine place. But closing sales requires you to show up with something more than you just being you. Being authentic isn't enough to close business and convert interested prospects into paying clients. Selling requires strong a skill set and a solid strategy.

For example, you may be the most authentic CPA, dentist, attorney or financial planner on the planet, but if you lack the ability to highlight your value and expertise or you are missing the skills that build confidence and trust in your buyer. I don't give a rip how authentic you are. Authenticity only gets you so far. I want to work with someone who possesses stellar skills in their field, skills that pair up nicely with authenticity.

What happens after you meet a potential client and you oozed authenticity? What occurs after a meeting when you were just being yourself and being real? Is there a stampede of people racing to hand over their checkbooks and credit cards? Or do you hear I need to think about it? I have no money. I can't afford it.

People often ask me if I can teach them how to sell with authenticity. My answer is that I can't teach anyone to be authentic. You are authentic, or you're not. What I can do is teach them the updated and evolved sales skills that allow them to show up as confident, and competent. I can teach them how to be congruent in what they say and do, which makes them authentic.

Anyone can make the claim that they are authentic, but showing up in a manner that is inconsistent with that claim, makes them look like a fake. No one wants to feel like they are being played by someone who is acting like they care.

Just because Pinocchio claimed that he was a real boy did not make it so.

In sales and life, you must be real. You must be yourself. You must show up as genuine. You must know who you are. When you are in a selling conversation or situation, don't just be yourself. Bring your highest and best self. Bring the self who owns superior sales skills and who understands how to genuinely build trust and honestly inspire someone to say yes to doing business with them. How refreshing is that?

Sales has changed so much over the past decade, yet sales trainers and gurus continue to teach strategies that were devised in a different time, for a different consumer. These gurus teach the miserable model from the 1970s that aggravates and irritates the modern buyer, who can spot these tactics a mile away.

First-rate sales rock stars are made, not born. Sales is a learned skill, not an inherited trait. Any skill can be attained, strengthen, honed, and enhanced, given the proper motivation and desire.

Business owners often declare, *I'm not a natural-born salesperson. I don't want people to feel like I'm selling to them. I am not comfortable with selling. I don't want to be perceived as aggressive, salesy, or phony.*

They express these mantras as a way of letting themselves off the hook of selling. They believe that if they think sales is evil or that they have to behave in a unethical way, they should have no part of it and will not participate in it. That is a surefire route to failure.

The way that you sell is always in alignment with your understanding and belief of what selling means. Let that soak in.

One critical aspect of sales is to sell with congruence. Your outer actions need to agree with your inner understanding of the process so that you feel true to yourself. It is only then that you will able to feel good about selling and cultivate dynamic relationships with people who want to buy from you. I can't think of a better way to build a business.

Has a colleague or trainer ever suggested that you try a sales technique that worked fantastic for them, but when you tried it you felt awkward and uncomfortable? Why is that? It's because they are not you. Those techniques are not parallel with who you are and how you want to sell. The words felt strange coming out of your mouth because they didn't resonate with your soul. They left you feeling like you were being inauthentic.

When a technique works well for someone else, it's because their values are compatible with the behavior required for that selling method. Since it didn't work for you, this is your body's way of telling you to find another way to say the same thing that feels good leaving your lips. Listen to your body. If something does not feel right, it is not right for you.

To most people the word selling conjures up images of the stereotypical, obnoxious individual who won't take no for an answer, someone who uses high-pressure gimmicks and cheesy techniques to close the sale. This person lacks the fundamental ability to sell value and resorts to such tactics to compensate for the fact that he lacks the skills to motivate a prospect to hire him. Traditional, old-school sales training methods are to blame for having perpetuated this perception.

Some professionals are pushy and antagonistic. They lie and manipulate. People like this may be found in every profession. If that floats their boat, so be it. But you don't have to engage in anything that resembles distasteful and offensive behavior.

A handful of individuals believe that if they vocalize their disdain for sales, they won't have to sell. That baloney only works until you run out of money, all while proving to yourself that you don't have to sell. If you can't sell in the 21st century, you are screwed. (That was my inner Jersey girl making herself known!)

Selling is at the core of every transaction in every industry. Sales skills are also relationship skills. Sales skills are fundamental business and communication skills. You can build your fortune as fast as you can build your skills. You control the financial faucet in your business!

On the flip side of those power-depleting declarations, I have heard other judicious individuals make statements of the opposite kind. *I know that if I don't embrace selling for my business, I won't have one. Selling is unpleasant for me, but I will find a way to enjoy it and appreciate the process. I know that I need sales skills to grow and thrive. If I don't know how to sell, I won't stay in business very long.*

Drop the negative energy and mindset related to the only thing that keeps your business alive and growing. You guessed it: sales. This negativity will no longer serve you on the pathway to profits.

Your transformation and re-invention requires a willingness to turn your back on what others may say, *That's the way everyone else is doing it. It's the way we've always done it.* You must be willing to create a breakthrough for your business. What used to work is in dire need of a makeover. It is imperative that you set traditional perceptions aside or erase them from your memory. When you do, you will never encounter a drought in your business again.

If you ignore the act of selling, you do so at your peril. Your business or practice won't last long if you can't bring clients in the door.

Sales And Selling Are Not Dirty Words!

Selling can be, if one so chooses, a high form of service from one human being to another. If you view selling as an opportunity to uncover needs and explore solutions, it generates a different atmosphere. If you discover that the client needs something that you can help him with, you discuss this in a heart-to-heart, collaborative manner.

Heaps of exceptional professionals use cutting-edge and non-sleazy sales methods to build their business. Shift your attitude that selling is improper, and instead think of it as helping people find solutions to their pain, problems, and challenges. Selling is about leading and moving people to action. You are the facilitator of that transaction. When others take action, you are compensated. Selling is about exchanging your value and expertise for money.

Only if there is mutuality of thought do you move forward. Mutuality means that the client is pleased with you and with the solutions that you have presented and that she wants to work with you. It also means that you are comfortable with her and would like to work with her as well. It is that easy.

This is no different than an architect drawing up plans for a home, a surgeon repairing a torn ligament, or a mechanic installing spark plugs in your car. Services are rendered for which money is exchanged. It is an easy, straightforward transaction.

Don't think for one second that if you are extraordinary at what you do, clients will beat a trail to your door and your phone will ring off the hook. If your compensation depends upon your ability to generate income and close business, at some point, you will have to sell. Sales corresponds to income!

Based on my research, most professionals don't sell well. It's true. Why? Because they have an erroneous view of what the selling process is. Most go about it the wrong way. They believe that they have to get someone to do something that they don't want to do. They think that they have to manipulate people to say yes to them.

People don't like to be sold to. They never have, they never will. No one, including you, wants to be convinced, manipulated, or persuaded. All anyone wants is support in helping them to make the right decision for them. Treat people like the human beings they are, and watch what happens to your bottom line.

Mastering interpersonal skills is critical to growing your business. The route to understanding how to engage buyers on a human-to-human level is also the avenue to wealth. Today's consumers are starving for authentic human interaction. They are hungry for someone to see them and hear them. The cheapest, most powerful way to connect with others is to do it with intention.

You have the ability to offer something that human beings most want from other human beings: well-sculpted people skills. These skills won't be going out of style anytime soon. Interpersonal skills are the key to creating value and converting clients. These abilities are atrophying in scads of people today.

Please know that you can be effective in sales no matter what approach you choose. Here's what I mean. You can use typical sales language that has been around for decades, you can apply pressure to get people to buy, and, of course, you could launch into a bunch of old-school closes that work from time to time, but they won't make you feel good about selling. And they sure don't make your potential clients melt in your presence. Or you can sell with honesty and integrity and engage in a way that makes people view you as a trustworthy advisor.

Selling is not something that you do *to* someone. It is something that you do *with* someone. The traditional way of selling is cold and impersonal. It undermines the building of high-trust relationships. It takes way too long. And it doesn't position you for referrals. This is not the way to earn trust, inspire people to hire you, and motivate others to introduce you to everyone they know.

Chances are that in your heart and in your gut you know that this is true. You may have always been uneasy with some of the tactics that you have used to sell your services, but either you didn't know what else to do, or you were doing what worked for someone else. Dishonest people exist, and there will always be unscrupulous individuals who do things for their own benefit. You don't have to act that way. You have a choice.

It is tougher these days to get your foot in the door and even harder to make your message stick in your client's mind. If you can't sell your services with some degree of consistency, it doesn't matter how grand those services are, you won't succeed.

Many of the thousands of individuals with whom I have worked came to me with a love/hate relationship with sales. They have told me that they love what they do but that they hate to sell. They love what they do, but they hate the process of finding new business. They love their client work, but they hate the idea that they have to sell themselves. To them, sales and converting clients is a daunting and unsavory task and something that should be shunned. Evading sales is a fatal business strategy.

If you are reluctant to sell or hate to sell, you are doing it wrong! This means that you have not found a way of selling that is comfortable for your personality and style.

Good sales skills will help you to close a decent amount of business, but strong sales skills increase your opportunities and help you generate more income.

Some people think that being good at selling means that you must be good at controlling, coercing, and manipulating people. For them, being good at selling means that you have to be good at being convincing and confrontational. To them, being good at selling means that you have to turn into some slick-talking, money-hungry sleaze-ball. That mindset is limiting your accomplishments and your income.

Being good at selling means that you are able to convey honesty, credibility, trust, and high value to prospects. Being good at selling means that you understand the dynamics related to how people make buying decisions. Being good at selling means that you talk about yourself and your services in a way that showcases your value and highlights your expertise. Being good at selling means that you may ask for the business without breaking into a sweat, heart pounding and knees knocking.

Don't run out of money and drive your business into the ground by demonstrating that you're not a natural-born salesperson. Think of it this way: when someone doesn't reply to your voicemails or e-mails, it doesn't mean that you are not a natural-born salesperson, it means that you haven't been taught the right language to use that makes people respond to you and communicate with you no matter what the outcome will be.

When someone thanks you for information, indicates that he will get back to you, promises that he will think about it, or tells you that he doesn't have the money, it doesn't mean that you are not a natural-born salesperson, it means that you do not yet possess the art of selling value. But it is possible to change this.

You Are Capable Of Learning A Progressive New Skill

You learned how to walk and talk. You figured out how to eat with a knife and fork, read and write, dress and bathe, drive a car. You didn't decide to continue to eat with your fingers, crawl on the floor, and wear a diaper because you weren't good at growing up. You acquired the skills that you needed to move to another phase of life. Now is the time to get the hang of the sales and conversion skills that will keep your business alive.

Building skills and habits that have numerous layers takes time. Selling takes practice. It also takes practice to set aside the sales behaviors that you've seen modeled by others and some of the habits you've attained.

It's like attempting to play a musical instrument or a sport. The more you practice, the quicker you will learn, and the better your skills will be. Those who choose to master the art of sales enjoy immense rewards.

You may find that your current mindset challenges you. First, you may tell yourself that you already understand an idea. If so, ask yourself if you just know it or are actually doing it. Have you imbedded this concept into your business? Knowing and doing are two completely different things. First you hear it, then you understand it, then you believe it, and then you do it.

When something becomes easy it's called a new skill. Pay attention to the difference between knowing and doing. I know masses of people who are heavy on knowledge and light on results. You can know something intellectually, but that doesn't mean that you can execute it effectively. This is just like losing weight. Everyone on the planet knows how to lose weight: eat less, move more. But few individuals actually succeed. Don't just know, do!

I read a study recently about what people want out of life. The majority of people want to be happy, healthy, thin, and rich. Some are willing to pay the price, but most want something for nothing. Well-crafted excuses wait in the wings about why these folks can't be happy, healthy, thin, and rich and why they lack the self-discipline needed to do everything in their power to achieve their goals.

Everyone knows how to be healthy: exercise, eat right, and get plenty of sleep. But the price is too high for some individuals, and their motivation is too low to make it happen. Everyone knows how to save money and build wealth, but the immediate pleasure of treating themselves to something that they can't afford is much more exciting. The only way to be happy, healthy, thin, and rich is to close the gap between knowing and doing and take action.

Do you cringe at the thought of repeating an activity that you find difficult or performing a task over and over again in order to perfect it? Developing a skill that doesn't come naturally to you may feel like a daunting task. You start the process but never see it through to completion because of a lack of self-discipline and because the chasm between knowing and doing is enormous. The task may have become too difficult to persevere, so you give up. When you lack self-discipline, it's easier to give up than to push through to the other side.

If you close the gap between knowing and doing, your life will be filled with any freaking thing you want!

Chapter 8

Overcoming Sales Rejection

Fear of rejection is one of the most common fears shared by all human beings. In small doses, we can all live with rejection. In large doses, it's the silent but deadly business killer.

Professionals suffering from fear of rejection sigh in relief and are elated if an appointment is canceled or a meeting is postponed. The simple act of picking up the phone, calling, or meeting a potential client is a gut-wrenching experience for women. Some ultimately fail because their fear has crippled them and does not allow them to move through the sales process with confidence.

Fear is like fire. When fire is uncontrolled, it burns up and consumes everything around you. When fire is controlled, it cooks for you and heats your home. When fear is uncontrolled, it engulfs you and will destroy you and your business. When fear is controlled, you feel better, you're prepared and positive.

Women who sell with a bone-shaking, knee-knocking fear of rejection have a difficult time earning the income that they desire and deserve. This strangles their businesses and chokes off success. Fear of rejection persists regardless of what these women sell, how well they've been trained to sell, or how much they believe in their products or services.

Some women are so clever at avoiding rejection that they'll do anything rather than put themselves in a sales situation. They declare that they're not afraid to sell, yet they dodge any activities that involve selling. They creatively evade any situation where they may have to step into the role of the salesperson for their business.

Fear of rejection never evaporates or disappears on its own. Selling with fear and operating a business with fear as the dominant fuel will put your business on a bumpy road, chock-full with potholes, ruts, roadblocks, and detours.

Fear of rejection is a condition for which there is no instant cure, patch, little pill, or quick fix.

Does the ability to handle rejection have a direct relationship to sales performance? Absolutely! In fact, an ability to handle fear is a critical attribute of prosperous female professionals. You were not born with the fear of rejection, so your learned fear can be unlearned.

Fear of rejection exists because of a lack of knowledge about how to sell effectively and a lack of clarity about the sales process. Fear surfaces because you're missing a certain skillset for selling. Having, knowing, and practicing these skills would make you feel confident and courageous in sales.

Scores of women have a fear of selling because they believe that they have to be someone they are not and that they have to sell out to earn the business. You don't have to be aggressive, have tough skin like a rhinoceros, be a fast talker, wear undergarments of steel, and have the teeth of a tiger to be good at sales. What you do need is to transform your view of sales.

The antidote to fear is the development of courage, character, and self-esteem, as well as good skills. Overcoming fear takes work on your part, but the rewards are sweet. I am pleased to tell you that there has not been one reported case of death from being rejected in sales!

Don't Take It Personally

How you handle rejection is simply a matter of perspective. Everyone gets rejected, and rejection stings. But rejection should only sting for a few seconds, like ripping off a bandage. Rejection is hard to deal with, but it is part of sales, part of business, and part of life. You shouldn't expect to do business with everyone. You will never be accepted by everybody. Don't take it personally. These potential clients are not rejecting you, they're rejecting your offer. If a certain situation is not a fit, it has nothing to do with you as a person.

Accept the fact that some people will choose not to accept your offer, because they don't see the value in it, they found another alternative, or perhaps it's not the right time for them.

People Can Sense Your Fear And Spot Your Weakness

When fear is present, your potential clients know it. As soon as prospects sense fear, they pull away and reconsider doing business with you. Your fear causes people to back away from you and not feel secure enough to buy from you. That same fear causes some people to ask for a discount. Fear makes smart people do dumb things.

How do you make purchases? You don't buy everything that you pick up and hold, try on in the dressing room, slip on your feet, drape over your shoulder, or inquire about. If it's not a fit, you say thank you and walk away. You're rejecting the object or the offer, not the person. Remembering this simple concept will help you view selling in a different light.

Fear of sales for a business authority is like a fear of the water to a lifeguard. Neither individual can be badass at their profession when fear is running the show.

Chapter 9

Show Up!

I witness professionals who focus on selling their company or their products or services but pay little attention to how they show up to sell and present themselves. Everything you say and every move you make either pulls clients toward you or pushes them away. Your words and communication style either attract or repel. You are an integral part of the package and part of what customers are buying.

Today's consumers are skeptical and don't put much trust in the words you use, so they look for other ways to gauge your trustworthiness. They assess you to determine if they can see themselves working with you. They evaluate how you make them feel and if you carve out the time to connect with them.

You may think that prospects are buying your brilliance, your reputation, your expertise, your prestige, or your high-end office space. Think again. It is you, baby, all you. If you want to know what your single most captivating competitive edge is, look in the mirror.

Do you have a sense of how other people view you when they first meet you? Are you transmitting subtle messages about yourself that convey anxiety, negativity, confusion, worry, desperation, or fear? Or are you broadcasting confidence, passion, trust, and accountability?

Business is not won at the end when you ask for the sale, it's won at the beginning when you show up in a way that conveys that you care and that you're there with your heart and your soul, not your head and your ego.

When you begin a client consultation, take your mind off of the end of the meeting. Take your thoughts off of any specific or desired outcome. Remove any thoughts about your quota, your bills, or your bottom line as you talk to a potential client. Put your focus on him, and get to know him as another human being. Stay in the present, manage the moment, and don't let your energy and focus get too far down the lane to closing the business. A lot has to happen in between *It's nice to meet you* and *Thank you for your business.*

I play a lot of golf, and in this arena I noticed a long time ago that I must manage the moment. I cannot be on the first hole and play well if I am thinking about and focusing my thoughts on the sand trap on the fifth hole, the water on fifteen, and the fast greens on eighteen. I stay in the moment, not thinking about or worrying about my future moves. When I manage my moments, I play better, and my time on the course is much more enjoyable.

When potential clients detect that you're starting a meeting or consultation with your energy centered around the intention of making a sale or landing a client, their guard goes up, they play their cards close to the vest, they withhold information, and they won't be transparent and truthful. Pay attention to your intention.

One analogy that I like to use in my training is that this is equivalent to showing up for a blind date in your wedding dress with your bridesmaids dressed and waiting in the car. You are concentrating on the wrong end of the date. You are not focusing on all the other stuff that must happen before you walk down the aisle.

When you arrive with the energy of wanting a specific outcome, you appear desperate and needy, and the client may sense an insecure vibe. The need to make the sale is the very reason that it is not happening. When people sniff a whiff of your neediness cologne or desperate perfume, whether mild or pungent, they will shut down because people are good at picking up on the intentions of others without trying.

You're sending out signals that you are there for the sale and nothing else. Prospects never buy in that situation. If people are not calling you back, not returning your e-mails, and otherwise evading your communication, it's because they read you correctly. This is the buyer's way of stating, *Get lost, move on, I will never do business with you.*

When you focus the spotlight on achieving a certain outcome, you lose authenticity and genuineness, and your consultation will self-destruct. Relax, be in the moment. Whether it is modest or glaring, people can feel your intent.

A Typical Scenario: You have the feeling that your meeting is going well, you think you have a good connection, and you sense that client engagement is high. The buyer nods and agrees with what you are saying. You may even be thinking that you just landed a client or feel certain that you will close the sale.

But the opposite is happening. You totally misread the situation. Your prospect can't wait to tell you that she needs to think about it, because when you first began the meeting she saw you as someone with an agenda and an intention that was focused on you, not her. The signals you sent out were focused on you and making the sale. People are smart and can spot and sense your agenda. This person concluded that you were not the type of person that she wanted to do business with, and the sale was lost in the first few minutes.

You receive back what you put out there. The problem is that most of the time professionals aren't aware of the vibes they're giving off. It doesn't matter how hard you work, it doesn't matter how good your product or service is, and it doesn't matter how good you are in the consultation. If you're broadcasting the wrong signals to your potential clients, you will not attract and do business with the type of quality and targeted clients your business needs.

Self-Assessment Time: When you begin any initial meeting or client consultation, do you display anxious, needy, nervous, or self-centered energy, or are you calm, real, poised, and cordial? Be honest. Check your energy at the door before you go into the meeting. Gather a sense of what you're feeling and what you're transmitting before you step into your next meeting or consultation with a new client. If the energy is off, change it. If your intention is wrong, correct it. If your mind is frazzled, calm it down. You are in control of how you appear. Are you showing up as self-centered or as your best self? Be honest, and make the necessary adjustments.

The Bottom Line: If you start a consultation with someone thinking that you must move them along your process, part of you will always be unfocused and nervous that if you don't follow the route that you set for yourself, you are not doing things correctly.

When you disconnect from your potential clients in that way, you convey through your words, the tone of your voice, and your body language that your hidden agenda is to make the sale. This backfires because today's perceptive consumers are familiar with this approach. They can tell when someone is trying to force them down an avenue on which they may not be ready to go, and they react with immediate suspicion and apprehension.

Distrust occurs in a split second, the moment someone's intuition tells them that although you appear to be attentive to their situation, you're leading the discussion toward a close. This is a slight form of manipulation that professionals engage in because they're fearful that if they don't lead people down their path, they might lose the sale.

Don't pull someone down your sales trail, allow them to walk down the trail with you. The only way to do that is to drop the hidden agenda, even if it is ever so subtle, and allow the prospect to travel to the end of the line naturally.

Aligning Your Mindset And Your Skillset

Books about how to sell fill libraries and bookstores. You may have participated in sales training or attended business classes that taught how to sell and how to be in business, the necessary external skills. They're terrific skills to possess, but you're on your own to gain the inner skills necessary in the game of business. If your inner game is off, you'll find it impossible to achieve the level of accomplishment that you desire. An out-of-alignment mindset will limit your ability to craft a robust business.

Many people fail for that reason. Their internal system (mindset) isn't congruent with their external system (skillset). Business owners know somewhere deep down that they have to sell, but their minds refuse to believe it. Their business is often heavy on the skills side but light on the belief, attitude, and self-worth side.

The inner mental game consists of your belief in yourself and your abilities. I'm talking about the internal dialogue that you have with yourself when you are alone. Your thoughts have more power than you think, and controlling the mental game is the toughest part of your business.

The outer tactical game of business consists of the actions you take and the skills you use to generate your results. It's the part of your business that the world gets to see. But if your inner game isn't congruent with your outer game, it is impossible for your business to grow or succeed. It feels like you are driving with one foot on the accelerator and the other foot on the brake. Your car may produce a lot of smoke, but you will go nowhere.

How The Inner Game Shows Up

Do you find yourself procrastinating and resisting things that are important? Have you ever sat next to your phone, making up excuses why you should not call people who would be perfect clients for your business? Do you want to make more money but find yourself evading anything to do with sales or following up? And even though you know that sales are part of every business, do you still refuse to sell? Have you cancelled a networking meeting for no good reason, knowing that it might make a huge difference to your income? That's the inner game you're playing, the game with no winner.

You may have at one time been or are now on your way to impressive sales skills, selling products or services that you believe in. However, in playing the inner game, your mind says, *I'm not a good business person. I don't have what it takes. Why would someone buy from me?* Your inner business person loses another deal. Making sure that your inner game is congruent with your outer game is the most important step that you can take toward triumph.

Once the two are aligned, you can untie the ropes and shake off the shackles that have kept you from building the success that you're capable of achieving.

The inner game is where the real work begins. Pay attention to what you are projecting and how you are showing up. Make sure that people move toward you, not away from you. The confidence that you project will inspire confidence in your potential clients.

Chapter 10

The Other F Word

Most people make a snap judgment in the first few moments (sometimes seconds) of meeting someone new. This is human nature, and we all do it to each other. *I like you. I don't trust you. I feel at ease with you. I don't see myself working with you. I feel safe communicating with you. I don't like your energy or tone. I feel good in your presence. I need to get out of here.*

Maya Angelou sums it up in eloquent fashion in one of my favorite quotes. *People will forget what you say. People will forget what you do. But people will never forget the way you made them feel. Feeling* is the other F word.

The mind of your prospect is deciding whether she *feels* connected to you and trusts you on the subconscious level. This happens in seconds and begins in the subconscious mind. It happens long before she is aware of how she feels about you on a conscious level. When people feel a connection with you, the likelihood increases that they will be open to holding a conversation with you. This is where either memorable or mundane first impressions begin.

In the first few minutes of any meeting, you connect with a person's instincts and their hard-wired reactions. Subconscious survival instincts kick in, and the mind and body decide whether to run, fight, or interact. Does this person offer an opportunity or a threat? Is he a friend or a foe?

This reaction isn't based on the specifics being shared in the words that you exchange. It has to do with how someone *feels* about what you're expressing.

A part of the brain, the amygdala, is responsible for that hard-wired instinct. Also known as the reptilian brain, the amygdala is an almond-shaped structure in the back of the brain that is defined as the fear center. Its primary role is to process memories and emotional reactions. It is an early warning detector, always checking our environment for anything that might harm us.

Your amygdala will recall if you have had a negative experience before, and these memories will be recovered and attached to what is happening in the present. The amygdala will yell at you, *Warning, you got hurt before. Be cautious. Don't trust this person. Remember what happened last time someone talked you into something you couldn't afford. Don't believe a word that this person tells you. This seems like a shady, too-good-to-be-true deal, run for the hills.*

Your prospect is asking herself, *Can I see myself working with this person? Will this person take good care of me? Can I trust his words? Are this person's words and actions congruent?*

You need to find a way to connect with the prospect on an emotional level. The best way to start the process is to get out of your head and into your body, or your heart. Speak to an individual's heart, not her head. When was the last time you had a heart-to-heart rather than a head-to-head communication with someone? If you communicate with your heart, this sends a message to the amygdala to relax its defenses.

I once attended a lecture about brain science and how humans make decisions. I learned about something fascinating, called limbic synchrony. Limbic synchrony is hard-wired into the human brain. Limbic synchrony is synonymous with mirroring, being in sync. We subconsciously switch our body language and posture to synchronize with the person with whom we are speaking. We sync up with that person's non-verbal behavior and signal that we are connected and engaged. We all do it.

Babies do it even before birth. Their heartbeats and body functions take on a pace that matches their mother. As adults, we do it when we are gabbing with someone that we like, are interested in, or agree with.

We've been harmonizing ourselves on the unconscious level with others since birth. Now it is time to do it consciously. The first moments of meeting someone have a huge impact on whether they will hire you. Your verbal communication is key, but your non-verbal communication is just as critical and should not be overlooked or ignored.

Non-verbal communication refers to the communication that occurs without using spoken language. Non-verbal communication, often otherwise known as body language, is principal in getting prospective clients to listen to your recommendations and hire you.

The message that you convey in your client conversations is 55 percent non-verbal communication, 38 percent tone of voice, and only 7 percent the words that you use.

Experts Identify Two Levels Of Communication

The first level of communication identified by experts is conscious communication. This includes words, writing, actions, and body movements. The second is subconscious communication, which includes the feelings, or the signals, that you send to the person with whom you are communicating.

We all know and have had those feelings when we are speaking to someone, and at some point we have thought, *I'm feeling a good vibe. This person makes me anxious. I feel like I've known this person all of my life. I want to run away.*

We all emit vibes and signals. When you're chatting with others and meeting prospects, you may do all of the right things, but if you feel something else on a subconscious level, nothing that you do will matter to your client. The reason for this is because as the old adage goes, It's not what you say, it's how you say it. If your words send one message and your body language sends another, the non-verbal part of the communication will win every time.

The feelings that you have beneath the surface are infused into how you articulate something, and the person with whom you're engaging can feel and detect this. People will use their gut and their intuition to make a decision, and much of that intuition is governed by what you subconsciously communicate. Don't underestimate the importance of this concept.

For example, you might verbally communicate, *I'm sure that this solution will fit your needs,* but your body language indicates, *I don't know that I can pull this off.* Your words do not match what your body reveals. Others feel this disconnect. When your words and body language don't match up, you lose.

Many times others don't know how they feel, or they can't tell you why they feel indifferent about you. They only know that on a subconscious level it seems that your words and your body language are incongruent. Something is off, but they may not know what.

People who do a poor job of reading their clients may be unaware of how their body language contradicts their spoken words, since the awareness of one's body language depends on the objective feedback of others. What is your body language communicating?

Chapter 11

Emotions Trump Logic Every Time

Buying is an emotional process, not an intellectual one, and this one idea is central to understanding what motivates people to buy. Buying and selling take place on an emotional level. Feelings trigger people to buy, act, and say yes. People buy, or not, because of their feelings. There's that good old F word again.

You may be the best and brightest person ever in your field. You may make every rational argument to demonstrate why it makes sense for someone to do business with you, but if you don't appeal to your prospects on an emotional level, you're just another person trying to sell them something. Don't delude yourself into believing that buyers make rational, logical decisions based on data, facts, figures, and information. That's not how the human mind works. Emotions come first, then logic. Emotions trump logic...every time.

Buying decisions are always the result of the consumer's emotional state. While information helps to alter that emotional state, it's the emotions that are vital, not the information. Don't undervalue the importance of emotions.

In your role as guide to the client, you must be willing to assist him with moving in the direction of seeking solutions to his problems rather than sticking with the status quo.

When you first meet a prospect during a meeting or consultation, her emotional state is often a negative one. She may be in any one of or all of these emotional states:

- Annoyed
- Scared
- Confused
- Angry
- Anxious
- Stressed
- Frustrated
- Worried
- Irritated
- Overwhelmed

As long as the prospect feels any of these emotions, she is not going to buy from you, be inspired by you, or do business with you. In order for her to consider your services, she must feel:

- Comfortable
- Confident
- Tranquil
- Relieved
- Safe
- Protected
- Motivated
- Content
- Satisfied

This means that it is up to you to shift the prospect's emotional state. Pay close attention to her. Observe how she reacts to your questions. Are the answers broad and elaborate or short and curt? Watch her body language, voice inflection, and eye contact. Listen for her emotional cues. Is she hiding her emotions and holding back information or being open, honest, and transparent? Be sure to have your antenna up during client conversations.

Why? When dealing with people, you are not dealing with creatures of logic. You're dealing with creatures with emotions. Neuroscience proves that people decide with their emotions and then justify their decisions with logic, without consciously knowing it. When there is no change in emotions, the prospect does not buy. This is where they tell you that they need to think about it or that they have no money.

Realizing that emotions always trump logic is an enormous component in understanding the buyer's emotional state and then helping him to move out of it and into a different, more positive place. This is done through the way that you interact, communicate, listen, and engage with others. Do you make people feel that you get them in such a way that you are the only person they want to work with?

Feelings are the fuel that prompt prospects to hire you. Logic makes people think. Emotions make people act. Stated another way, logic makes people need to think about it. Emotions make people hire you. This will always be the way that people make buying decisions. This is the same way that you buy.

Sure, logic will be a tiny part of a buying decision, but the primary decision to buy is driven by emotions. Take the time to tune in and turn on the emotions in your prospect.

People who don't feel their own emotions will never touch emotions in others. But a keen professional knows that people buy with their emotions, and they are willing to go there with a prospective client.

Some individuals will argue this point to the death because they're apprehensive about the notion that they must access prospects' emotions. Like it or not, that's the way it is. It's reality. Arguing with reality prevents professionals from earning a sizable income. I tell my clients that the journey is a short one. It is eighteen inches from the head to the heart. I encourage you to take the trip from logic to emotions.

Not convinced? For the next few days I want you to be an astute observer. Every time you see a commercial or a magazine ad, ask yourself which feeling it is selling.

If we take the example of pharmaceutical commercials, we see that a white pill helps you sleep, a purple pill relieves heartburn, a pink pill alleviates allergy symptoms, and a little blue pill allows for four hours of sexual enjoyment. These commercials don't mention the company that makes the pills. They don't talk about how long the company has been in business. The viewer of the commercial is not told about ingredients in the pills, the shape or the size of it, or about the proper dosage. No, commercials tap into the emotions and sell the feeling of being alive, energized, healthy, motivated, sexy, refreshed, and ready. Advertising agencies know that the consumer is in a negative state, and they are selling the consumer on how he can get to a positive and happier place.

These commercials are designed to grab the attention of the consumer and sell to the feelings of the unconscious mind. They sell the emotions of what happens after you swallow that pill, and that's what motivates people to buy. Have you ever taken a pill to feel worse? Of course not.

Still not there? Are clients and opportunities disappearing before your eyes? You know what I mean. You may have thought that a prospect was guaranteed to hire you, but she changed her mind at the last second. Perhaps you were working on a promising deal when with no explanation, the opportunity spins out of control and is lost.

You're certain that you have connected and communicated with the prospect. You clarified everything that your prospect needed to know about your services, and he has a sufficient budget. You tell yourself that it's in the bag and high-five yourself in your mind.

Then out of nowhere, you hear something like, *I liked you and will give it some thought. Your presentation was incredible. We'll keep you in the loop. What you have shared makes a lot of sense. Let me run it by the others. I need to think about it, and I'll get back to you.*

Why does this happen? You may have attempted to inspire someone to buy from you using logic, not emotions. Logically it sounded like a good idea to the buyer but emotionally not so much. On the rational level your services made sense to her, but she was not feeling the connection. Logic cuts off possibility. Emotions open up opportunity. Make people feel something! Sell the feeling!

Chapter 12

People Always Buy You First

People really do buy people. You could be a stellar professional with premier services and an impeccable reputation, but what matters most is how clients perceive you and how you engage and communicate with them.

When a customer makes a buying decision and chooses to work with you, generally it's not because you have the best product or service, the lowest price, or delivered the best presentation. Your customers buy from you because they like, trust, and believe in you. You first, everything else next!

If you want people to trust you, and then hire you, dazzle them by taking the time to connect with them and show them that you're a human being just like they are.

Prospective clients do not hire you solely because of your expertise. They hire you because they feel that you understand them on a level that other experts do not. Never underestimate the enormous value that prospects place on beginning a business relationship with someone who is sincerely focused on helping them.

Don't hold back. Let them see the real you. Allow yourself the freedom to show off your personality and style. Showcase your sense of humor. Demonstrate your soft side. Reveal your resilience. Be vulnerable. Display your compassion. Exhibit your poise. Give prospects a full picture of your abilities and personality, and allow them to make the decision about working with you.

Offer prospects a glimpse of what it would be like to work with you. Don't hide who you are and then do a classic bait and switch. Meaning, don't pretend to be one way to get the business and then swap out your real self after you close the sale.

Example: I met with a tax accountant who appeared, on the surface, to be organized and efficient. When I arrived to meet her, her office was neat and tidy, and I felt secure in her abilities, so I hired her. Three weeks later I had to drop off some paperwork. I called her to say that I was twenty minutes early and that I could run up then. She invited me to come on up to her office.

I walked into her office, and it looked like a tornado had blown through and annihilated her office. She apologized for the mess, and I left with a bad feeling in my gut. I knew that I could not work with her. I was honest and told her how I felt, and she understood. I now have a new tax accountant who has paperwork all over her desk, but she owns it, and she knows where everything is.

You are often the differentiating factor in a prospect's decision to buy. While fees, delivery of service, and the solution itself are significant, what makes a prospect choose you over your competitors is you.

Sales is, and will always be, about people selling to people. Somewhere along the line business became about business rather than about people. Selling is about relationships. Your best deal-closing tool is and always will be you. You are your greatest asset.

Where Are You On The Empathy Scale?

In the execution of your business you have practiced numerous skills and featured lots of your excellent qualities.

You have shown clients your persistence, patience, creativity, trustworthiness, tenacity, honesty, reliability, and integrity. While all relevant, one influential element of achievement in all types of relationships is empathy!

One of the skills that top female professionals use that converts interested prospects into invested clients is their empathy. Empathy is needed in today's selling environment. Empathy is an active force.

Empathy begins with self-awareness. To become effective at tuning into the emotions of others, you must first become capable of tuning in to your own emotions and acknowledging your emotional blind spots. We can all be more empathetic with others, so this may take practice and deliberate intent at first.

Empathy is the ability to step into someone else's situation and experience emotions from their perspective. Empathy is understanding another person's feelings and using that understanding to guide your conversation. You demonstrate empathy for people by identifying with them on an emotional level. Empathy involves the ability to emotionally understand what another person is experiencing.

True empathy sends a potent message that sounds and feels like this:

I appreciate where you're coming from.

I can see how you could feel that way.

I relate with what you're feeling.

I've been there before and wondered the same thing.

I understand why that would have upset you.

What you're saying is quite common and makes sense.

You are acknowledging how someone feels in that moment. Most likely you do some of this without much thought. How about today you do this deliberately and wholeheartedly with good intent?

Empathy is the yeast of a conversation. Without yeast, the bread that you are baking falls flat. Without empathy, you may find your conversations falling flat as well.

Build your empathy skills. Clients like it when you have empathy. It reassures them that they have selected the right person to hire or do business with. Empathy is the key to emotional intelligence.

Beware! Although being empathetic is one of the keys to selling your products or services, this trait may also hinder your influence. Too much empathy may hurt you. If you are too empathetic, you'll say things that make you sound weak like, *I don't want to bother you, but your invoice has not been paid. I hope I that am not imposing on you, but I need... I don't want to hurt your feelings, but... I know that you're busy, so I won't take up too much of your time...Did I interrupt anything?*

Wipe all of these sentences off the slate. Delete all of them and anything else that resembles them. They do nothing but strip you of your confidence, authority, and selling abilities.

Chapter 13

Genuine Connection Is The Pathway To Profits

In the last few years the quantity of online interaction has skyrocketed, and the quality of good old-fashioned human connection has plummeted. An immediate and widespread flood in personal interaction is the antidote to this sorry state of affairs. And now is a darn good time to start interrelating with purpose and intention. Human connection is the fertile soil in which relationships grown and flourish.

Your goal is to make a connection. Connection is not about superficial small talk. The connection step makes people feel that, in this moment, they are the center of your universe.

Have you ever set out to buy something, found what you were looking for, at a reasonable price, and didn't purchase because you didn't like the person selling it? My guess is yes. Sometimes it's not your product or the price that determines whether you get the business. Sometimes it's simply the way that you connect or don't connect with people.

Connectability equals profitability. Connection is and will always be a critical and fundamental human need. Connection creates comfort, establishes trust, and builds buyer confidence. If you don't connect with others, it will be difficult to convert someone from an interested prospect to an invested client.

The most insatiable human need is the feeling of significance or importance. Connection is about making someone feel as if they're the only person in the room. Every time you have a conversation with someone new, you have one primary goal, which is to make the other person feel calm and at ease in your presence.

Please don't be one of those people who pretend to be interested in someone or who whips out some artificial authenticity to be used in the moment. That junk can not only be seen, it is felt. If you have to simulate authenticity, you may want to consider a job where you don't have to deal with human beings. If you connect from your heart and talk to people with genuine interest, you will leave a lasting impression on their heart and mind. No joke, this being sincere and real thing works. I dare you to try it and mean it with the next ten to twenty people you meet.

The practice that I choose to use when meeting someone new is this. From the moment I meet someone, I look for something positive that I could say about them. I check out their eyes, their hair, their physique, their nails, their personality, their smile, their dress, or any number of other things about them that I could compliment. I say something nice about that feature to myself. It helps me to think kind thoughts instead of leaping to the judgmental thoughts to which we all have a habit of going. When you look for the good in people, you always find it. Focus on the good, and the connection is felt.

When teachers build an intentional connection with their pupils, learning happens. When doctors make a deliberate connection with their patients, healing happens. When companies have an intended connection with their clients, business happens.

It's easy to fall prey to the misconception that the ability to connect with others is a natural but unteachable trait, that the ability to connect is something that you were either born with or not born with. The truth is that this ability is within your control. Anyone may turn a superficial dialogue into a genuine connection. Anyone may turn shallow chit-chat into a meaningful discussion. You just have to be willing to shift the dialogue to another level.

Real connection is significant and often overlooked when meeting with prospective clients. You've most likely felt that type of connection with someone, when you walk away from a heart-felt and generous conversation feeling lighter on your feet. You might reflect to yourself, *I feel like I have known her for years. I could have talked to him all night. It was so easy to converse with her. He really made me feel better.*

People value and pay more for the way that you connect with them and make them feel. I know this because your prospective clients have told me that in many cases they hired a professional whose fees or prices were a bit higher but that they liked the way they were spoken to and how they were treated. Quite a few people whom I interviewed told me that in the first three minutes of the consultation, they made up their mind that they were going to hire the expert that they were meeting with even though they had no clue what their rates were. I heard dozens of stories that support the notion that people pay more for the way that specialists connect with them and make them feel.

It's hard to influence people without first making a personal connection with them. Why should a prospect care about your input or what you think if you don't take the time to connect with him? He will tune you out. He may nod, listen a bit, but in the end, the connection is weak, and you will hear, *I have no money. I need to think about it.*

People may listen with their ears, but they make choices based on how you make them feel. Their brains are trying to connect with you, and if they do, the likelihood of them making a buying decision in your favor rises. If they don't like how you make them feel, you will come in second and send another first-rate client to your competition. Don't let an additional five or ten thousand dollars fly out the window.

Have you ever given much thought to how people feel when they interact with you? Have you ever thought about what people experience being your presence? Are you approachable and user-friendly? Have you ever taken the time to consider whether you're truly connecting or whether you're just going through the motions?

The only conclusion that a prospect's unconscious mind can form is how relating with you makes her feel. How does your presence, personal energy, and connectivity make others feel? In her book, *My Stroke of Insight*, Jill Bolte Taylor writes, *You are responsible for the energy you bring to every situation.*

We are all responsible for the personal energy that we bring with us. When I say energy, I am not referring to indulging in frenetic activity or speaking with enthusiastic verve. I mean your personal and centered energy. I mean being at ease, approachable, calm, focused, and transparent. Your personal energy relates to your connectability.

Your prospective clients will form an immediate impression of you based on superficial observations, but most won't make up their minds until you open your mouth and show them who you are. That's when they form their second impression, which is based on your ability to connect intentionally. And that impression may certainly decide the fate of the sale because, in most instances, a client's second impression supersedes the first one.

Some of my favorite skills that I teach in my programs, and some that other coaches and consultants don't, are the most potent and intoxicating of all. They are soft skills!

Soft skills is a synonym for people skills and interpersonal skills. The definition of soft skills is this: personal attributes that enable someone to interact effectively and harmoniously with others.

Soft skills have nothing to do with being weak. They have nothing to do with being quiet, proper, passive, docile, spineless, well-mannered, or any other word that means the same thing.

Professionals who have honed their people skills close more business and retain more clients. They know that it is these skills that give them the best leverage and an enormous advantage over their competition. They have a mighty secret weapon and are not afraid to use it with precision.

Research conducted by Harvard University, the Carnegie Foundation, and Stanford Research Center revealed that 85 percent of success comes from having well-developed soft skills, and only 15 percent comes from technical skills and knowledge, hard skills. Being excellent at what you do is appealing, but being brilliant at connecting with others is priceless.

Notice for yourself if your soft skills need a mini repair, a modest rehabilitation, or an extensive renovation.

Using soft skills means being able to transmit sincere interest, authentic compassion, bona fide connection, and heartfelt empathy to prospective clients. Individuals with excellent soft skills are able to have an honest and open interaction with others. They are aware of what their body language communicates. Soft skills are what top women professionals use to tip the scales in their favor and produce more profits.

When you embrace and master soft skills, you and your business will never be the same. Using interpersonal skills will have an enormous impact on your business or practice. Those who have supreme people skills generally also have a high level of emotional intelligence. These are the unbeatable skills that change the emotional state of a potential client.

Do you know someone who seems to connect with people no matter the situation? What gives them the ability to carry on dynamic conversations? What is their secret? They have remarkable people skills.

For some people, soft skills are often the hardest skills to develop, perhaps because interpersonal skills necessitate that you get out of your logical thinking (your head) and drop into your emotional feeling (your heart).

Soft skills are the new differentiator for professionals. Don't expect potential clients to mention that your interpersonal skills are smooth or that your soft skills are sophisticated. Something much more momentous is going on.

Prospects won't be able to put their finger on or identify any words relating to the difference. They will only know that in your presence they felt heard and seen. They may even think to themselves, *Hmmm, she is different. I feel connected. I like his style. She is sharp, and I respect her polished and professional manner. He communicates in a way that fits me. This is the right person for me.* Your soft skills pack an undeniable emotional punch and will always serve as a strong differentiator.

I am reminded of a morning when I was leaving a meeting with a new client.

Angela strolled with me to the elevator. "I admire your approach. I talked to three other consulting companies, and I feel like you were the only one who took the time to understand me. You seem to really enjoy the work you do, and your passion is contagious. I'm ready to learn how to sell from you and thrilled to have my associates work with you."

Her words spoke to my heart.

Caveat #1: Be aware of what may get in the way when attempting to connect with another human being. One epic thing that keeps us from bonding with other people is our inner voice or our inner critic. We listen to that voice instead of the person that we're talking to. We're thinking about what we're going to say next while the other person is speaking. We're so focused on the inner voice that we fail to hear what is being communicated to us. The words come through loud and clear, but the message is lost.

Your inner critic is always asking and answering questions. *Is this true? Is this false? What's the problem? What's the solution? Should I do this? Do I like her? Do I agree? Do I oppose his views? Does this make sense? Can I see myself honing this skill? Is her proposition even possible? Do soft skills matter? How am I doing with my interpersonal skills? What's in it for me? How much longer is this going to take?*

Stop the madness! Pause and notice some of the exchanges that you have been having with yourself about what you're reading right now on the pages of this book. You'll hear your inner critic in action.

Your inner commentator runs so constantly that you may not notice it. Listen to what your internal voice screams or whispers. Is it constructive or destructive? If it is destructive, turn the volume way down on your inner critic.

Caveat #2: Another hidden trap that undermines your ability to convert prospects into paying clients is your desperate need to retain a new client or close the business. This trap may damage the integrity of the meeting or consultation. The ego-driven need to win, although quiet, may also be quite dominant.

As a result, you may attempt to convince a prospect to hire you. In reality, you are trying to control the other person's decision-making process. When that happens, all of the things that everyone abhors about selling come into play: control, manipulation, pushing, coercing and all of the other elements of outdated, traditional sales tactics. Even if you are doing this at the lowest level, any attempt to manipulate or control a client's behavior is a lose-lose proposition. This causes buying resistance on the part of the client. The more you try to convince her, the more she resists.

You may be thinking, *Aren't I meeting with this prospect because I need a new client? Aren't I supposed to try to close the business? Isn't that what this entire meeting is about?*

Yes, closing business and acquiring clients is the optimal outcome. But trying to snag the prospect as a client is attempting to control his behavior. This damaging zeal to *close the business* may lurk under the surface of a conversation. This wanting to secure a new client runs in the background of your mind. Regardless of how loud it is, it is there, and a prospective client can pick up on it.

When you attempt to control someone else's behavior, they resist. This scenario plays itself out every day in typical consultations and meetings in conference rooms all across the country. Every time you try to press for the close, this produces pushback and resistance. If you lean in, the prospect pulls away. It feels more like a sales arm wrestling match. The client may feel like you are stepping on the accelerator instead of coasting. It's astonishing how much more business you can close when you stop pushing for it and trust the process and yourself.

Caveat #3: Another snare in which we get trapped is that we think that we must change who we are when we are around different people. Good people skills are about being consistent. You are the same person with the janitor as you are with the queen. Pay attention, and check to see if you are wearing one social mask with one person and a different mask with another.

Soft skills require a lot of practice to become adept at using them. No assessments exist to prove that you have mastered soft skills. You measure your success in developing soft skills in how well you manage your relationships with those around you, how you relate to others, how you move a prospect from interest in you to investing in your services.

Chapter 14

People Skills In Action

People will not trust you and relate to you unless you intentionally connect with them. They will not listen to you until they first feel heard. People will not hire you unless they feel that you *get them* and take the time to understand them on a level that others with whom they meet are unwilling to do. Once you form a solid connection, this makes the process much more pleasing for everyone!

This process takes no more time than what you're doing already, but it will serve you well. Let's review an example of two different approaches used by two financial planners:

Financial Planner #1: Brian meets with Brenda for an initial consultation.

He greets her in the lobby. "Hi, Brenda, come on back to my office. How was the traffic? Did you have any trouble parking? Please make yourself comfortable.

"Now, before we talk about the reason why you are in need of a financial planner, I want to tell you a little about myself and how my process works. I've been a certified financial planner for twenty-two years. My firm has more than forty-four years of combined expertise. Financial planning is in our blood, and we take superb joy in helping our clients. At this firm, we pride ourselves in treating each client with the same care and respect that we would offer to our friends and family. I have a flawless reputation. So what brings you in today, and what can I help you with?"

Financial Planner #2: Alison meets with Brenda for an initial consultation. She greets her in the lobby and is upbeat, unguarded, and warm. Brenda notices and feels something different in Alison's demeanor.

Alison is focused on Brenda. "Brenda, thank you for coming in today. I'm glad that we could meet to discuss your situation.

"Brenda, I've had a chance to read through the information you sent over last week, and I know a bit about your current circumstances. Before we dive into the specifics and the finer details, I'd like to know if anything has changed since our brief conversation last week."

Alison allows Brenda to share her initial thoughts and offers her empathy. "Thank you for sharing, Brenda. I understand that initial meetings like this may feel stressful, strange, and nerve-wracking. I will have to ask you personal questions about your financial condition and how you got into your current situation.

"I believe that knowledge is the key to making informed decisions, so I am here to help you in that regard today. My goal is to make sure that you leave here today with the information that you need to make a decision about hiring a financial planner to assist you with your investments. Our meeting should take forty-five to sixty minutes. Does that work for you?"

Allison gives Brenda a chance to respond and listens to her.

"Brenda, after going over some of these particulars, then we'll discuss what it would look like to move forward and begin the process, if that makes sense at this time."

What happened?

Financial Planner #1: Brian instructed Brenda to get comfortable instead of taking the time to help make Brenda comfortable. He chit-chatted about the same shallow and inane things that most other professionals talk about. Brian attempted to bond and create rapport by asking insincere and generic questions about the traffic and parking.

He chose to begin the meeting by fixating on himself and his firm rather than on Brenda. Brenda had to wait for him to end his monologue so that she could move to a dialogue about what matters to her. Except that the monologue never turned into a real dialogue.

Brian also asked the same lame questions that so many professionals resort to. *What brings you in today? How can I help you?* Those are the same questions that I am asked when I shop at Home Depot. You can do better than that.

Brian blew it. He did not put Brenda at ease and make her feel like she was significant. He failed on several levels. His people skills were non-existent.

The story of Brian is an example of a typical initial client consultation, not a personal and memorable experience. At the end of the meeting the client pronounces in her head, *I am not sure that I have the money. I need to think about it.* Brenda never calls Brian back.

Financial Planner #2: Alison took the time and care to design a trusting and safe environment in which honest communication could occur. She walked into the meeting open and kind. She took the time to put Brenda at ease and allowed her to get comfortable. She eliminated all small talk and chit-chat and opened the consultation with meaningful and emotional conversation.

She used Brenda's name four times and wanted to know how she was feeling. Alison made Brenda feel important and not like just a number. She made Brenda feel like she was in good hands to open up. She put her strong people skills into action. Alison showed Brenda that she is warm and compassionate.

She gave her the opportunity to speak first, knowing that when a prospective client talks first it can be calming and soothing.

The first thing you say to someone in a consultation is the most critical part of your exchange. Your opening comments set the tone for the rest of the conversation. It is up to you to observe the person that you are meeting with and tailor your comments to him.

Your job is not to push someone down your sales path. Your job is to open every client interaction by being gentle and inquisitive. Be deep and clear like water.

Both of these financial planners were capable of handling Brenda's monetary needs. Both had the expertise. However, only one specialist used her upgraded people skills and her knowledge to connect with Brenda.

Keep in mind that the prospect may not consciously know how or why you are different to her. Her gut and intuition tell her that you are not like the other professionals with whom she has spoken. These feelings happen on an unconscious level, which, by the way, is the level on which people make buying decisions.

Every initial meeting or consultation should open with your customized opening statement. Failing to begin a meeting with your personal statement will result in lost opportunities and revenue. Neglecting to set the tone and intention of a meeting may lead to a meeting that goes off the rails and becomes burdensome to salvage.

Top professionals know that in the first few moments, they never talk about themselves, their credentials, or their company. Allow prospects to draw their conclusions about your competence and credibility by how you behave instead of by what you tell them. You will have plenty of time later to discuss who you are and how you can help.

As you adopt this soft skills approach, clients will recognize your ability to understand their issues and their goals. Prospects will view you as a trusted professional who is focused on their needs and is capable of providing solutions.

You move from being an adversary to becoming the prospect's greatest advocate.

One of the splendid facets of using soft skills that makes your meetings and consultations so effective is that rather than delivering a monologue about you or your company and the value that you bring, the client experiences your value by seeing the relationship that he will have with you. As trite as this may sound, actions do speak louder than words.

A client's direct knowledge of your value and capability is worth infinitely more than you trying to convince her with words. She does not have to speculate or wonder about what it would be like to work with you. She feels it and sees it first-hand.

Superior people skills shift the entire dynamic of the meeting and build a phenomenal foundation for a relationship to begin. With this approach, you become a model of trustworthiness and professionalism to your prospect.

Some professionals have pushed back against this concept. *I don't have time to hone my people skills. I'm busy, and it seems like I would have to go to a lot of trouble to learn something new. I would rather get down to business and make the best use of my time. I don't do emotions and feelings. Prospects are going to like me or not. Prospects can take me or leave me, I don't care either way.*

What these people are saying is that they don't have time to pull out their people skills and have a heart-to-heart conversation. They don't have time to construct a new way of conducting a meeting or initial consultation. They are making it about themselves. These people wonder why they do not stand out, sell themselves, and close more business.

This is remarkable news for you because your competitors, who don't use their soft skills, won't get the business, you will. You know that your soft skills are the secret weapon in your arsenal. You know that this secret weapon goes with you everywhere you go, on every call you make, and to every meeting in which you participate.

Think of a time when a professional, such as a CPA, website designer, dog walker, book editor, consultant, or surgeon, awed you. What did that person do to engender a positive feeling in you? Did you perceive a high degree of expertise, sincere concern for your circumstances, and a display of empathy? If so, you felt high trust and were amenable to sharing information.

To attain that level of trust, that professional had to know how to conduct a client consultation. You must do the same. Find your unique style and a communication approach that will make you stand out. Otherwise, you will blend right in with your competitors.

No matter what type of client situations you face, you need to know how to execute a persuasive and profitable initial meeting or consultation. I call this the *win or lose* interaction, the *deal or no deal* consultation. It is the conversation that encourages prospective clients to listen to you and consider hiring you or back away and head to the competition.

The people who make using soft skills look the easiest work at it the hardest. Achieving a dependable level of skill takes practice as well as real-world encounters. Just as you can't learn to play soccer by reading a book or become a master chef watching cooking shows, you won't become adept in the essential people skills necessary to lead sensational client conversations without practice.

Keep in mind that the opening or beginning of the conversation is unique to every professional and every prospect. It is up to you to conceive a captivating opening that differentiates you from your competitors. It is critical that the words in the opening feel right to you and that they flow in a way that is in line with your communication style.

A tremendous opening paves the way to a favorable closing. An unproductive opening paves the way to prospects leaving your office underwhelmed, discouraged, and unwilling to hire you. The opening serves as a game-changing differentiator.

One of the elements of my business that has become quite popular, and one that I delight in doing, is what I call the *Mock Consultation Evaluation.* My clients have found that conducting a simulated consultation is the most cost-effective way to pinpoint the expensive mistakes that send top-notch clients...and profits...to the competition. My clients realize enormous value in rehearsal and role-playing. Rehearsal is the quickest route to consultation mastery.

As a skill-boosting and growth-building tool, role-playing instills know-how and certainty and prepares people to be proficient in client interactions. Evaluating a consultation is an indispensable tool that identifies skills that are weak and need urgent resuscitation.

If you were an attorney, you wouldn't think about going to a court hearing without being sufficiently prepared. Yet, when walking into an initial consultation, many specialists do just that. Broadway actors attend dress rehearsals to ensure that opening night is astonishing and entertaining for their audience. You can do the same.

The skill of conducting a stellar client consultation is overlooked by most people. They continue to focus much of their money and their efforts on marketing or lead generation, mistakenly thinking that this will solve the issue of declining profits. It never does. Why keep throwing money at the problem of lead generation/client attraction rather than investing in the skill that converts those leads into paying clients?

Most individuals believe that they're pretty good when it comes to their skills in the consultation. In my research I heard everything from the ridiculous to the sublime. *I suck at consultations. I'm okay, but I'm sure that I'm not perfect. I think that I'm doing all right, but I resist doing things all the time. My consultation skills are fabulous, but I hate asking for the business. I do an excellent job, except for when it comes to talking about money and my fees.*

I understand that no one wants to admit that they don't know how to connect, communicate their value, discuss fees, and close a deal, but why be marginal when you could be magnificent? The *Mock Consultation Evaluation* is a low-cost investment that produces a speedy return on that investment. It's an easy solution to an expensive problem. It is what one of my clients called a *no-brainer*.

Warning: Simply changing your language as seen in the Financial Planner #2 example will help you to stand out, but your words alone won't create the magic. What creates the magic is what you infuse into who you are, the feelings that you arouse in the client as you deliver your words. There is much more to the opening than what you express that will alter how your prospective client sees you. Your intention, mindset, eye contact, body language, tone, and word choices matter just as much.

I work through this crucial exercise with every client. We formulate the language, test it out, and ensure that the words come out with rock-solid confidence and land with impact.

It is necessary at the beginning of a meeting to set the right tone and intention because this is the part of the meeting that elicits the most resistance, pushback, and opposition from prospects, as they don't know what you intend to do to them. They think that you are going to try to close them, push things forward, and go in for the kill. They are in protection mode.

An opening statement may be crafted in dozens of ways. Make it your own. Choose your words with care. If your statement sounds like a series of canned words coming out of your mouth, the client will hear it and feel it. If your statement sounds robotic and scripted and does not come from an authentic place, you are finished.

There is no standard approach. Each client is so different that to expect one approach to work for every one of them is unrealistic.

Below is a high-value bonus snippet of information. What is the one word that you can use with all of your current and prospective clients that will ensure that they notice you?

What one word can drive your business through the roof? The answer: your client's name. It is her favorite word.

Everyone Loves To Hear Their Own Name

When you address your client by his name, it not only personalizes your conversation, it shows him that you are paying close attention. When you use your client's name, you will keep his interest. Don't overdo it, though. That makes it weird.

Reflect on this old aphorism, spoken by Dale Carnegie, *There is no sweeter sound to any person's ear than the sound of their own name.*

When you use a client's name, you break down a lot of barriers that may block communication. You position yourself for a better relationship with your client. Plus, this helps you remember and identify your clients. It's easier and kinder to acknowledge someone when you use her name. You don't want to blow it at the end of an engrossing conversation and have to say, *Remind me of your name again.*

Chapter 15

Listen Up! Your Ears Are Your Money-Makers

Good listeners make more money than good talkers. Listening is a foundational skill of all professionals and the key skill to becoming superb at client conversion. Listening is the skill of understanding customer needs.

Stephen R. Coveys proclaims, *Most people do not listen with the intent to understand, they listen with the intent to reply.*

One of the supreme gifts that you can give someone is to listen to them and remain present. Listening takes concentration and a desire to understand the other person. Incredible listeners have the ability to make others feel understood and recognized. They give the impression that they have all the time in the world to have a conversation with you. Giving someone your full attention, listening to what is being said, and resisting the urge to be thinking of what you want to interject next is easier said than done.

Contrary to popular belief, selling isn't a career for people with the gift of gab, it's for people with the aptitude to listen.

Have you ever noticed that the same letters that make up the word L-I-S-T-E-N also make up the word S-I-L-E-N-T?

Silence draws people out. It's in the silence that you get the answers you need.

Listening is the one tool that everyone can further develop, yet it's the one skill that plenty of individuals spend little time working on. Observe where you spend most of your time, and focus on how much you listen. You will be amazed how much your business and your life will improve when you listen to understand.

Listening is not only a skill, it's a habit of good communication as well. Through the process of listening, you enhance your communication and allow less chance for misunderstandings and mix-ups. More notably, you give the other person respect and validation. What a glorious foundation for a wonderful relationship, a sense of shared understanding.

Could you listen at a deeper level? Could you open your ears and shut your mouth? You ears are a considerable asset in your business. The part of the conversion process that can make or break a sale is not hearing what your customers say. If you ask questions of your potential customers but do not pay attention to the answers, it will cost you income.

Notice how you listen when you are with people. Pay particular attention to how you are focused on the other person, as opposed to being mentally distracted.

Some individuals are often accused of talking too much, and there are a variety of reasons for this. Some people are nervous because they lack the solid sales skills necessary to inspire a client, so they think that if they keep talking people will eventually say yes. Others think that they know more than the customer, so they lecture him. Lots of professionals feel compelled to recite their canned pitch regardless of the buyer's actual interest.

The key to connecting with a client is through conversation. The secret of an awesome customer conversation is to ask questions, and the quality of the information received depends on the quality of the questions. Learn to listen, even pausing to wait for further comments.

Nobody thinks that they're a poor listener. In fact, most people think that they're a good listener and tend to overrate themselves on their listening abilities. I know I did.

Not listening is an occupational hazard. Curbing the urge to talk is a behavior worth mastering. Some people come across as a know-it-all. There isn't a question that they can't answer, there isn't a problem that they can't solve. The difference between being a know-it-all and being a source of knowledge depends on how and when you share your knowledge. It has been said that *buyers don't care how much you know until they know how much you care.* Listening may fall into one of the categories listed below. Which one do you do most often? Do you even know?

Active Listening: Active listening is a way of listening and responding to another person that improves mutual understanding. You listen to content and intent. You try to block out barriers to listening. You are non-judgmental and empathetic.

Inactive Listening: Inactive listening is being present when someone is speaking but not absorbing their words. You hear the words, but your mind is wandering, and no communication is taking place.

Selective Listening: Selective listening is hearing what you want to hear or what you expect to hear instead of what is being stated. You hear some of the message and rush to formulate your reply or second-guess the speaker without waiting for the speaker to finish.

Reflective Listening: This is one of the most complex types of listening. It involves active listening, interpreting what is said, and observing how it is said. You work to clarify what the speaker says and make sure that there is mutual understanding.

A lot more goes into listening than just keeping your mouth closed. Listening and asking questions establishes a positive relationship and builds trust. When you let clients speak and you really pay attention to what they say, they feel recognized and heard.

A high price is paid for poor listening skills. To listen takes concentration, hard work, patience, and the ability to interpret your customers' words and summarize them. Ineffective listening may damage relationships and undermine the trust that you have with your clients.

It is not possible to multi-task and speak and listen at the same time. If you're jabbering, you're not listening. This rule also applies to the chatter inside your head. If you're thinking about what you want to say next, you're not listening to your client. Listening costs you nothing, but not listening costs you the sale and income.

Like any new habit, this one will take time and practice before it becomes second nature. Try it out on your next consultation, on a date, or around your spouse or kids. You will find that you will be able to close more sales more quickly if you listen rather than if you talk.

Listed below are 5 levels of listening. From which level do you listen?

Level 5 - Not Listening/Ignoring

I'm sorry, what did you say? Tuning out, pretending to listen, thinking about something else, and not paying attention all fall under this syndrome. If you're going to tune out or ignore, try tuning out the outside distractions and your internal dialogue, and listen to what others are verbalizing.

Level 4 - Listening To Tell Your Story

You think you've got it bad, let me tell you what happened to me. You broke your leg in two places? Well, I broke my foot, and I broke both arms to boot. This is an annoying habit. This happens when you're not listening to what the other person is saying. Instead, you're taking that time to prepare your own remarks. The intent is to share how your story relates to the other person's for your own self-satisfaction, not for understanding and learning about someone else.

Level 3 - Listening For Judgment/Assumptions

Here's your problem. This is where you make assumptions and come to conclusions before you hear the whole story. As soon as you hear a potential customer say something specific, you leap in to offer a solution. Once you reach a judgment, you are no longer listening.

Level 2 - Listening For Application

Tell me more. Being able to listen to and understand what you may take away from another person's comments requires the suspension of assumptions and judgment. You lean in and listen harder. This skill is useful in groups of people who gather to learn from each other.

Level 1 - Listening For Understanding/Clarity

So what you're saying is... Level 1 is the highest level of listening, listening to understand and gain clarity. When we listen to understand, we're listening authentically, not automatically. We really hear what someone is conveying.

Just like any skill, listening takes practice. You must spend time refining this worthwhile skill so that it pays dividends in business and in life. If you are proficient at listening, you will build high levels of trust with your clients.

Shut your mouth, and open your ears! Remember, good listeners earn more money than good talkers.

Pro tip: Want to show someone that you care about what they are sharing? Take notes. Jot things down. Plus, writing down important information helps you recall the full content of the conversation. Show the prospective client that what she contributes matters.

Chapter 16

Differentiate Or Perish

Lousy news alert! Today's consumers believe that you are just like your competition. Yep, they really do. Consumers, in a number of industries, have told me that they can't tell one professional from another because they all look and sound identical. All marketing material and websites look comparable. Prices and fees are similar. To the customer, it appears that you do the same work, you provide the same information, and you offer the same value and expertise. There is nothing unique or special about what you do.

You are the only one who can change that. The time for innovation and differentiation is now. Those who stand out get noticed and hired.

What once gave professionals a competitive edge no longer does. Technology is accelerating change at an ever-increasing pace. Technology has lowered barriers to entry, and this is allowing for a cornucopia of *comparable* competitors.

Standing out in the prospect's eyes is a reason why she will choose you over your competitor. The more you telegraph what makes you the better option, the more often you will be a customer's first choice.

To stand above the crowded marketplace, you must offer your prospect a unique and distinctive benefit or advantage above and beyond that of your competitor. If you don't, people have no incentive to do business with you as opposed to others in your industry.

When it comes to the present, one thing is certain. Your prospective clients are on the hunt for an expert who is choosing to utilize a fresh approach and explore innovative ways to stand out in the host of service providers out there.

A major danger to your business right now is not being able to define what sets you apart in a world that is cluttered, competitive, and crowded.

One of the best opportunities to differentiate yourself in today's world is through your approach, through how you show up, connect, engage, and communicate.

These days it is not enough to be brilliant at what you do. It is not sufficient to provide an excellent service. Today you also must have additional assets. Have you identified your edge? What sets you apart from your competitors? What value do you provide, and how is it different than the alternatives?

The competitive environment that you face today is much more intense than in the past. It has never been more challenging to find new business. The changes are so significant that your company won't survive without differentiation.

If you choose to stay where you are and continue to look and sound like your competition, you are making a conscious choice to languish in irrelevance.

To gain a substantial advantage, you must be different from your competitors and different in a way that makes a difference to your prospective client. Otherwise, you will fall head first into the commodity trap.

Some individuals complain that clients view their products and services as a commodity, leading them to ask for discounted fees. If clients indicate that they can't differentiate your services from those of others, what they're vocalizing is that they can't see that what you deliver is different than what your competitors offer.

Now the commodity game begins and shifts the encounter to something that people may differentiate: your pricing and fees. You can escape the commodity trap with the ideas and the value proposition that you present to the client. Differentiate yourself from your competition by demonstrating to your prospective client that you bring more to the table than your competitor.

Every professional in every industry brings something different to the value table. The burden of proof is on you. You can't count on prospects to identify on their own the value that you bring to the table, to calculate what your services are worth, or to determine if they should pay your fees.

Many individuals have a tough time answering these questions: How do I stand out from my competition? How are my products or services different from those of the last few people that a prospect talked to? Why should a potential client hire me instead of the firm down the street?

Some profess that what differentiates them is where they attended school. Others proclaim that it is how long they have been in business. Some think that it is the prestigious firms where they have worked. Some assert that it comes down to their mission, vision, and values. All of these humdrum things are now monotonously pontificated about on websites and blogs throughout the universe.

Some business owners answer the *how are you different* question like this:

- I have been an accountant for more than twenty-three years and have an excellent reputation in my industry.
- I am proud of my practice and the exceptional services that I provide to all of my clients, during what may be an emotionally challenging time.
- I take the time to listen to you and understand your needs.

Prospective clients have also heard this: *Our firm opened in 1966, and since that time, we have been the best provider of accounting services in this area. Our staff is knowledgeable and qualified. Our fees are competitive, and we pride ourselves on the service that we deliver to all of our clients.*

What the prospective client hears is an advertisement about how marvelous you are, not how what you do delivers value to him. Your answer is stock and standard and generic and boring.

After reading or hearing these statements, how do you feel? Interested in hiring this professional on the spot? Eager to retain her services? Nope. In fact, none of these people have told you anything that you didn't already expect to hear or read. You've probably heard it all before, from umpteen other similar professionals or on their websites. Tell prospects what they can't read on your website or social media profile.

At this point, the prospect has no way of differentiating one professional from another, except a gut feeling and, you guessed it, fees and price. Distinguishing your services from those of your competitors will result in wins for you. Failure to differentiate yourself results in a direct comparison. The business owner with the lowest price wins the business.

It's a race to the bottom when you look like everyone else. Why wouldn't a client go with the lowest-priced company? When you haven't made the case that you are better than the competition, that's the situation you will be in.

It is often this lack of differentiation that makes clients shop price. Your fees may be the only difference that prospective clients see.

Other professionals answer the *how are you different* question this way:

- I have decades of experience that you can trust.
- We provide one-on-one attention to all of our clients.
- I am committed to building long-term relationships.
- Our company is dedicated and loyal to our clients.
- I treat every customer with care and respect.
- Our team pays special attention to the fine details.
- My expertise is the best in the state.
- We care about your financial future.
- I am committed to walking you through the process.

- We protect what's most priceless to you.
- I take the time to listen to your needs.
- We put our clients first, and they are number one in our eyes.

Yawn! These examples are not unusual. Statements of this kind are also splashed in bold letters on websites the world over.

Your statements about how you are different are irrelevant to prospective clients. Using statements that are predictable, over-used, and unoriginal is not differentiating yourself. There's nothing unique and nothing distinct about them. They promise no added value. This is the equivalent of shouting, *Hey we are just like everyone else, but I sure hope you give us a chance to prove that we are not.*

None of the above statements offer even a scintilla of uniqueness. These declarations cause you to blend in with your competitors. They do nothing to highlight what makes you special. Every single one of them is a baseline expectation for prospective clients.

Let's imagine that a prospect asks you why you are different, perhaps in the middle of a consultation or at the end when she is making a buying decision. She is not asking for the answers that you typically give. It is a bit of a trick question. She wants to know how what you do differently affects her. She wants to know that it relates to her, how it adds value to her, what it means to her personally.

I will give you an example of what I say and what I teach, but I urge you to put some thought into the statements that you make about how you're different.

I teach my clients how to differentiate themselves by using language that the client has already shared and loop it back to him.

If Mary, a prospective client asked me, *Liz, why should we hire you as a consultant to train our staff rather than any other trainers out there? Why are you different?*

Mary might expect me to proclaim, *I have been an expert in the sales communication industry for more than twenty-five years. I deliver outstanding results with all of my programs. I can double or triple your business revenue in six months or less. I adore what I do and the difference that I create for my clients. My reputation is on the line, so my clients are my number one priority.* This hollow answer is known as lip service.

These over-used claims would be generic and expected. These basic and boring statements don't cause someone to see me as different. All Mary hears is a giant justification as to why she should hire me.

But if I want Mary to hire me, I might state, *Mary, that's a valid question. I know that some of my competitors might do a few things the same as I do. Some of them teach sales and communication skills to a broad range of professionals. However, my style and systems are quite unique. Earlier you mentioned that you were not at all interested in investing in an off-the-shelf or generic one-size-fits-all program for your team. You wanted to invest in something new, fresh, and updated. You wanted something modern and contemporary that would help your people be more effective when selling their services.*

My consulting services are distinctive because I not only teach people how to sell themselves and their expertise with confidence, I invest additional time in helping them understand the psychology around why people buy and what they need to make buying decisions. They learn about themselves, and they understand the consumer. This leads to converting more interested prospects into invested clients.

Mary, you also mentioned that you don't want your people to use or rely on word-for-word scripts that sound robotic. Some other consultants lean heavily on using generic scripts that work in other industries, but generic scripts make it much harder to stand out. I customize the process and utilize language that fits your team and the culture of your business. Then we test it and modify it to ensure that it is working and that your people are using it. I don't believe in cookie cutter language.

Then I stop and check for understanding. *Mary, have I sufficiently answered your question?*

Pause, take notice, and see where this is going. I tied the question of how I am different back to something that the prospect told me in our initial consultation. If I spring into a stock answer, I will have wasted the opportunity to stand out.

Mary may reply, Yes, *Liz, you hit the nail on the head. We don't want to use a generic and standard script. We have to do something different to stand out. The competition is growing, and coming in second will not cut it anymore. We want your help in forming a more modern way to communicate with our clients.*

I know that I did not reply in the way that Mary expected. My answer was what she needed and valued hearing. People don't want me to launch into a speech about how terrific I am and all the wonderful things that I can do. I handled the *how are you different* question by addressing the concerns that Mary shared with me throughout our meeting. I answered the *how are you different* by being different. You can do the same thing.

Shifting your approach will not only make you stand out, it will also increase your bottom line. It did for me. I know that I win more business because I know how to be distinct. I know that that distinction serves as value, credibility, and a trust-builder.

Bite down hard on your tongue if you feel compelled to dispatch a common, insincere, and unoriginal response to a prospect's concerns. The professionals to whom I have taught this concept tell me how refreshing it is to answer the *how are you different question* in a way that doesn't make them justify or validate who they are. This approach has tremendous value for them.

The more your language caters to what's in it for the prospect, the more proficient you will be at capturing her attention and maintaining her interest. *It is all about her, it is not about me.* This is your new mantra. Repeat it one hundred times.

Prospective clients filter your words through their perspective. Think about how you plan to articulate important information about you, your services, your firm, and how you are different. Prospects need to hear you and feel what you say.

Take the time to drill down and develop a message that sets you apart.

Do the following exercise, and give this critical aspect of your business some consideration. Spend time thinking about what makes you distinct. Ask others what they think makes you unique. Everyone has a differentiator, so don't let yourself off the hook until you discover yours.

Listed below are some questions to ask yourself:

- What is my unique offering to the marketplace?
- What are my distinct characteristics, areas of expertise, skills, and attributes?
- What is the look and feel of my brand? (If you get stuck on this one, I suggest hiring a branding expert.)
- How can I integrate that uniqueness into all of my messages, promotional materials, writings, speaking engagements, and services?
- Once defined, how can I make my singular traits recognizable in a stable and sustainable way?
- Who is my main competition?
- How is what I do different from what the competition does?
- Who do I know that could give my firm and me an advantage in the marketplace?

Define your difference now. Not tomorrow, now! Not when you get around to it, now! Not when you're in the mood, now! Not when your plate isn't so full, now! Not when your schedule clears, now!

You can thank yourself later!

Chapter 17

Value Is Far More Critical Than Price

To separate yourself from your competitors, you must construct an environment in which the prospect can see the value and the expertise that you provide. If your prospects can't otherwise discern value, they are going to use the one measure that makes sense to them, your prices and fees.

The concept of delivering value is one of those things that is both simple and complex. It is elementary because delivering value does not have to be grand or expensive. It is complicated because value may only be identified by the client, because different people place significance on different things and to different extents.

What's valuable to one person might not be prized by another. Things are valuable if they are appreciated by that particular client. What you think you are worth and what others think you are worth may not be the same. What you think should be meaningful and cherished may not in any way be significant to your client.

If a client informs you that she is going with a competitor who has lower fees, she is telling you that she does not see enough difference in the things that are of value to her to pay the difference in price. This is no different than buying a computer, a boat, an appliance, boots, or home furnishings. If all of the choices appear to be the same, why would someone pay more?

Did you really lose the sale and the opportunity because of your fees? Let's first address the issue of when it is about the money. If your prospect does not have sufficient funds to hire you and does not have the financial means to pay your fees, then yes, that is a fee issue. There will always be people who cannot afford your services.

However, if your prospect has the financial ability to hire you, this eliminates price as a reason for choosing your competitor. If he has the money to hire you but chooses not to do so, then money is not the issue that is driving his buying decision. Value is the underlying driver.

Why did you lose that client and that opportunity? You lost it because, after weighing both options, the prospect did not see enough difference in value between your services and those of your competitor to justify spending the additional fees. This has nothing to do with your fees. It has everything to do with your failure to differentiate your value proposition in a way that matters to your buyer. Value is personal to each prospect. The more you state your value in terms of how the prospect wins and how she profits, the more it will be perceived as real value.

Until you find out what each individual values and speak to that, you will always be beaten out by someone with a lower price.

Differentiating yourself and your services from those of your competitors will result in steady wins. Failure to differentiate yourself results in an apples-to-apples comparison in which all options being considered appear to be the same.

In the absence of perceived value, almost any product or service may be driven down to one thing: price. If you deliver value, you will never have to compete on price. Don't allow price to become a default position. Don't allow your fees to be the only point of reference available for separating one option from another.

It is your obligation as the business owner to help the potential client make a well-informed decision by showing your value as it relates back to him.

Value is the difference between the fees that you charge and the benefits that your prospect perceives that she will derive. If your prospective client sees that she will receive an extensive benefit for the price that she pays, then her perception of value is high. You control the dial on this perception of value. The more you focus on the value that you deliver, the less significant price becomes to the prospect.

When you add value, you provide the prospect with something that he is not expecting. You offer him something that makes him view you as distinct, not like all the others. It is up to you to know the value that you bring and what is esteemed by your clients and speak to it.

Value is in the eye of the beholder. No matter what you believe about the worth of your services, it is the client who decides the significance of what you provide. The client is the final arbiter of value.

Given the competitive nature of business, how do you separate yourself from all of the other options? How do you show a prospect that you are not like any of the other professionals being considered? How do you provide the type of value that would make a prospective client pay higher fees for your expertise?

Showcasing value is accomplished by how you position yourself and the type of questions that you ask. The questions that you ask and the way that you ask them will allow the client to step back and see his situation or business from a different perspective. The client is going to gain new insights and understanding about the obstacles that she needs to deal with.

You tip the value scales in your favor because you are the trusted advisor who helped the prospect see things through a different lens. You shined the light on something that he did not realize or think about.

You communicate to the prospect in a silent way, Regardless of whether we end up working together, you will get value from our interaction. You will leave here today with something to think about, something that piqued your interest, something that shook the status quo.

It is a common fallacy that people buy based on fees or price. Some do, of course, but most people buy based on value or their perception of value. Some business owners open their doors with the thought that they will enter the market and offer what they have at a lower price and that their business will do fine. They soon see how false this assumption is.

Prospective clients are afraid to part with their money. Money equates to security, and it doesn't matter whether you're asking someone to part with $195, $1,995, or $19,995. People are happy to spend their money when they see that there is more value in using your services than there is in keeping their money.

In almost every buying situation, the prospective client visualizes an imaginary set of scales in her mind. In the decision-making process, the prospect uses those scales to weigh the value of the product or service being considered. What happens in too many cases is that professionals do a lousy job of presenting the specific value of the service that they offer. They fail to show the client how she will be much better off after procuring their services.

When this happens, the value of what you bring to the table is not seen. Your clients get their value scales out and determine the benefits that they would receive versus the money that they would be required to spend.

This is the moment where the weighing game begins in your client's mind. He weighs things out to see if value does exceed your fees and if the benefits outweigh the cost. If so, you win the business. If not, you start all over with another prospect.

If the prospective client feels that what you offer is what she thinks she can get from a less expensive expert, she will not do business with you. She perceives the value in your offering as similar to your competitors.

People don't always buy based on the lowest price. No one believes that the lowest price ever equals the best quality. You don't win clients, opportunities, and business on price. You win them on the value that you create. Consider that if price was the only thing that mattered and people were looking for the least expensive options, everyone would drive a Kia, Nordstrom would be void of customers, flying first-class would take a nosedive, and we would all drink Folgers coffee.

Selling on price alone is a losing proposition. Show prospects the value in what you offer, and price objections will disappear.

It is imperative to understand what your clients value before you can give them that value.

I have listed here several ways to add value to what you offer: your pleasing personality, offering a guarantee, speedier service, payment options, addressing your client's true needs, providing different levels of service, increasing your agility by adapting to changes in the client's circumstances, the manner in which you keep clients in the loop, being on time, your willingness to customize your services, taking the initiative, bringing new ideas and insights to the table. And the best way to add value, a classic, is to under-promise and over-deliver.

Figuring out this value stuff is hard, and there is no one right answer for everyone at all times.

Take the time to find out what your clients value and give it to them. But don't stop there. Give them some of what they didn't even know they wanted. This is the jolt that leaves clients with that WOW feeling. But there is still one more critical piece to adding value.

Features And Benefits Are Good, But Show Me The Value

No doubt you have heard about features and benefits selling, a style of selling that was in vogue in the 1970s and

1980s. If you are selling features and benefits, it is time for an update. Features and benefits selling is in dire need of a funeral. I suggest that you find a shovel, dig a gigantic hole, and bury this sucker forever. Nothing will make you look more archaic than omitting the value part of the conversation.

A feature is an attribute of your product or service and describes an aspect of it. A benefit is the outcome or result that users will experience by using your product or service.

Feature: This home is located on a cul-de-sac.

Benefit: It is in your preferred neighborhood and close to the elementary school.

Feature: These tires come with traction control.

Benefit: Your car will grip the road better.

So what! Big deal! Show me the value and how that value relates to me.

The only way to show that you care is to ask quality questions, listen to the answers, and then connect the dots between your product or service and the buyer's unique needs.

People will tell you what's important to them if you listen to them. Without finding out what someone values through listening, you are merely telling them what you think is of value to them. Find out what matters to the buyer and what they value when making a buying decision. Value is specific to each individual. Value exists in the mind of the evaluator.

Value sounds like this. Let's use the home buying example.

Feature: This home is located on a cul-de-sac.

Benefit: It is in your preferred neighborhood and close to your children's school.

You could state the feature and benefit in a stale way like this: *Pamela, this home is located on a quiet cul-de-sac and is a stone's throw from the kids' school.*

Or you could jack your value up and explain it in such a way that Pamela knows that you heard her concerns and understood what she truly values.

Value: *Pamela, you shared with me your concern about not buying a home on a busy street because you have three young children. Because this home is tucked away on a quiet cul-de-sac, you will feel safe when the kids are outside playing, and you won't have to worry about traffic or distracted drivers. The nice part about this street is that the people who drive on it are mostly the people who live here. Plus, it is close to the kids' school, so if they have to walk to or from school, the road is less traveled.*

A buyer might say, *Absolutely, I am concerned about safety. You're right, the traffic has gotten so congested around here in the last few years. I have enough to worry about with the kids playing outside, let alone having to watch for cars.*

It is up to you to hear what Pamela mentioned earlier. You must connect the value dots for Pamela. Pamela dropped her value bomb that she required safety and proximity to school in her new home. These things were her driving factors in purchasing a home. Pamela might have thought about the safety concern, but when you bring it back it and tie it into the conversation, you convey that you listened to her and that you care.

Many professionals fall into their own trap, believing that what they sell is valuable. It is not, not until your potential client recognizes that value. Your perspective implies that everyone should recognize the value in your product or service, and that is not possible, nor is it realistic.

There is no better way to reveal how much you care than by understanding and responding to your customer's unique needs and what he personally values. This is different from pitching generic features and trying to turn them into common benefits. Personalized value makes all the difference. If you offer this kind of value, it is the best way for you to look modern and knowledgeable. Value can't be generic, and it can't be mechanically and mindlessly built into your client conversation. You must do this with every buyer, in every consultation, every time.

Adding value, talking about value, and conveying value doesn't come from a one-size-fits-all script. It has to come from caring about your potential client. Caring about the buyer means that you want to understand and care about her enough to offer solutions that will solve her unique problem.

Bake this skill into your bones, and your meetings, consultations, and conversations will never be the same. Join the ranks of the top professionals who do this with every client they meet.

Chapter 18

The Trust Factor: Get It And Keep It

Much has changed in the world of business, but some things have not and never will. Building trust was essential five or six decades ago, and it's just as crucial today.

Trust is a must. Trust is paramount when building business relationships and keeping loyal customers. Without it, you don't have a prayer of landing the business. With it, you'll have an opportunity to construct a profitable business. Be mindful that before you establish trust with potential clients, they're going to be suspicious of your intentions. Why? Because of the professionals and salespeople who lied, misled, convinced, and talked them into doing things that they did not want to do in the past. Unscrupulous people did what they needed to do to get the sale. Your buyer's guard is up, and only you can take it down.

Trust is the foremost indicator of buyer behavior and one of the key components to establishing effective business relationships. Trust is demonstrated and reinforced one discussion at a time. Trust is comparable to super glue, which forms an unbreakable bond.

Making a connection and relating to your customers in a way that is genuine is an impressive way to generate trust.

If building relationships is the key to victory, then trust is the foundation necessary in erecting those relationships. Today's consumers are busier than ever and have access to more information and more choices. They're looking for someone in whom they know they can put their trust and who will do the right thing.

The building of a relationship with a client is not a separate activity that takes place before or after a meeting. It is inherent in every meeting or consultation and beyond.

Most new client interactions begin with high tension and low levels of trust. Moving your prospective client from a low-trust, high-tension level to a high-trust, low-tension state is essential. When you reach a level of high trust and low tension, your prospect stops resisting and begins to see you as her only choice.

We all buy from people whom we trust. We are all influenced by people whom we believe. Make building trust a priority.

Knowing how to develop sincere trust is essential to boosting your bottom line. Trust is the single most important prerequisite for creating client relationships that produce monumental results with less time and effort. Earning and maintaining trust must be approached with deliberate intent.

When someone wishes to speak to you, you've gained their interest. Next, you need to earn their trust. Then, if all goes well, you secure their business.

When buyers have faith in you, they feel comfortable and confident that you will do what you say you will do when you say you will do it.

When you care about people, when you want to help them achieve their goal, you have an advantage right from the start. When you truly care, your reputation will precede you.

Trust does not depend on the length of time that two people have known each other. Trust depends on the depth of understanding that grows between them. Your reputation for being dependable is something that you strengthen over time with a consistent, positive performance.

Your prospects are coming to the table with less trust than they did in the past. These days some specialists make promises that they don't keep and say that they will do things that they never do. The bar on trust is set low, and you can work to raise that bar. In the old days of selling, professionals asked for trust, and that was enough. Not anymore!

Your clients will likely decide within the first few minutes of talking to you whether you're the type of person with whom they want to do business. We size people up based on the way that they communicate with us, and we do this swiftly. It all comes down to whether someone trusts you.

You may be the most honest person on the planet, but if your clients don't perceive you to be trustworthy, it doesn't matter. Do not announce that you are client-focused, be client-focused. Do not indicate that you are always on time, be on time. If you say that you will respond to someone in twenty-four hours or less, respond to her in twenty-four hours or less.

In today's competitive marketplace, your clients have untold options, and they're looking for someone who walks the walk and talks the talk. Being conscious of this will help you to solidify a firm foundation from which you can conduct your business.

Knowing, understanding, and possessing the traits that clients need is the best way to attain trust and seal the deal. In addition to being honest, you need to be knowledgeable, punctual, solution-based, and customer-focused. It's the way that you relate to others that determines your client's level of trust.

Before you pick up the phone to call a prospect or sit down to an initial meeting with someone, make sure that you plan to earn trust with intent. Make sure that you will be able see things from the client's point of view. Your prospects should leave a meeting with you thinking, S*he is a fantastic listener.*

She can help us with our business issue. She put me at ease, and I can see myself working with her.

If you keep your prospect's needs in mind, you will both walk away from a meeting in a better place. All parties are happy.

Rapport And Trust

There is a fine line but a clear distinction between rapport and trust, but this is often missed by inexperienced professionals. Understanding both will put you in a stronger position to convert more clients.

Rapport has three components: compassion, connection, and credibility. Think of each of these concepts as a building block in the foundation of your business success. Rapport sets the tone of the relationship between you and a prospective client. Rapport is a feeling of shared trust and a sense of harmony with each other.

Trust also has three components: competence, commitment, and consistency. The taller the building, the deeper the foundation required. That means delivering on your promises.

Each time you do this, the foundation becomes more solid. Trust translates to a prospect having confidence that you will do what you say you're going to do.

Think of this as it relates to the dating world. You meet someone for the first time. You notice that they're working way too hard to impress you and get you to like them. They agree with everything you say, look you in the eyes while smiling, and hang on your every word. This overkill is freaky. It's too much too soon, and trying too hard is a glaring sign of desperation. This approach ends up backfiring because forcing rapport and trust feels unnatural.

It's hard to trust someone when they are trying too hard. On the flip side, when you meet someone for the first time and things are going well, the atmosphere feels friendlier and more peaceful. You almost start to feel the trust emerging, and the banter flows light and easy. Rapport must be forged at the beginning of every relationship, whether it lasts twenty minutes or twenty years.

Think of a time when you met someone for the first time and the conversation felt natural, comfortable, and tension free. You could see that you were a good fit. Or recall when you met someone, and the conversation was heavy and unpleasant, and it felt like you were sinking in quicksand.

When was the last time you made a sizable purchase from someone you didn't like? When was the last time you gave money to someone you were not so sure about? Chances are, almost never. The same is true for your clients. Just because someone likes you doesn't guarantee you a sale. Gaining trust and building rapport with your clients when you move through the sales process will help you close more sales.

You will no longer worry about your consultations because you'll know where to keep the focus, on your potential client. This builds trust and causes your fear to evaporate. Your comfort level increases, and you come across as loose and cool. Your conversations become trust-filled dialogues that make it easier for people to open up so that you may gather the truth about their situation. When you set aside your own agenda in the conversation and focus 100 percent on your potential client, trust grows, and the truth emerges. What an incredible way to begin a business relationship and an astonishing way to sustain one.

Chapter 19

Not All Prospects Are Worth Pursuing

Learning to qualify prospective clients is a challenge for all professionals today. Qualifying a lead may be the difference between closing a sale or chasing people who can't or won't make a decision. Your chasing days are over for good.

Pursuing potential clients to close a sale has always been an element of old-school selling and the traditional sales mindset. *The more I follow up, call, e-mail, and chase, the more I increase my chances of making the sale.* This implies that your primary goal is to make the sale rather than focusing on whether you can help a potential client with her challenges.

You can be the utmost authority the world has ever known, but if you're dealing with someone who is not authorized to make decisions, or talking to people who are unwilling to engage and make a commitment, you're wasting precious time and wearing out your expensive running shoes chasing someone who does not want to be caught. These people are unqualified, and you must move on. Let them go!

Don't deceive yourself or get into the habit of believing that everyone you encounter or speak to is a potential client. Don't think that everyone wants and needs what you're selling.

The responsibility of qualification falls on your shoulders. It is up to you to evaluate whether a real opportunity exists there. As a professional it is up to you to determine if this potential client would make a good client. Maintaining control of the consultation and asking the right questions (more about this in the next chapter) will weed out prospects who are mildly curious, truly serious, or who have no potential at all. It's up to you to find this out sooner rather than later.

If your prospect meets these three key criteria, she is a qualified prospect:

1. Does the prospect have a need and true aspirations to fix his problem? Does the prospect need your product or service now or in the near future? It's up to you to be inquisitive and ask questions relevant to that need , uncover his pain and his challenges, and it's up to you to discover if he is serious or curious about finding a solution to his problem. Serious people are ready to tackle their problems. Curious people enjoy talking about their problems with no intention of fixing them. Spending time with curious people is a colossal waste of your time. Don't assume that someone is ready to move into action because he is talking to you.

2. Does the prospect have a sufficient budget? A qualified prospect has the money to purchase your product or service. Don't squander time pursuing someone who truly can't afford to buy what you sell. If a potential client has $500 to fix a problem for which you charge $5,200, you must walk away or refer her to someone else. This person is not a fit. You may suggest other options, but do not exhaust yourself pursing this type of sale.

This is true for any business or any industry. If you blow the transmission in your car, you might go to the repair shop with $450 in your pocket, but if the mechanic charges $4,700 to repair your Lexus, he won't do it for you. Asking about budget early in the process allows you to find out whether the person you are speaking to has any money to spend, and if so, how much. Don't be abusive or rude when inquiring. Ask in a way that serves both parties.

Sometimes people are embarrassed to ask the tough money questions. Don't be. You can't do your job if you don't know the prospect's budget, and you may be wasting your time if his budget isn't sufficient to pay your fees.

3. Does the prospect have the authority to buy? A strong lead and a qualified prospect is empowered and prepared to take action. He is ready to go from interested in your product or service to invested in your solutions. He is done talking about his heartaches and is ready, willing, and able to take action. He can write the check, and he has the power to say yes.

Without all three of these ingredients, a sale is not likely to take place. There will always be people who are interested in what you do and sell. There will always be people who only want to talk about their problems and have no intention of correcting them. We all know people who love to talk about their trials and tribulations but who have no plans to take the steps necessary to address them any time soon.

Chapter 20

Asking Better Questions

Much of the advice offered today that has been written about asking questions is archaic. Today's consumers are much more sophisticated and won't put up with simple-minded questions like, *What keeps you up at night?* They won't tolerate manipulative questions such as, *If I could show you a way to increase your online presence would you do business with us today? If there was a way to help you to get healthy and reduce your body fat, would you be open to trying this product? If I could do X, would you do Y?* Asking questions such as these is the oldest sales trick in the book.

To be successful at client conversion, you must approach your customers with a series of direct, specific, impactful, and potent questions that ensure that you understand their struggles. Asking questions is vital to finding, qualifying, and closing business, as well as offering the best possible solutions for your potential clients. Being inquisitive swings open the doors to a deep understanding of your buyer's situation.

Critical in sales and client conversion is understanding what your buyer's answers mean, not just what they say. That's why a fact-finding mission on your part is essential to uncovering your prospect's real challenges. High-caliber questions reinforce your credibility as a trusted advisor and expert. They validate your understanding of her issues, and they are how you get to the root of the problem, not just the symptoms.

In order to present your solutions, you first must learn what your customer needs. This may seem obvious, but some business owners are oblivious to this type of questioning.

You may be thinking, *But I do ask questions. I inquire all the time. I have a list of strong questions.* In my work with thousands of professionals, they don't ask as many meaningful and well–crafted questions as they think they do. What they do instead of ask and listen is *tell.* They ask a question and then go into *telling* mode. They explain all the ways that they can help, fix, or solve someone's problems.

For example: A potential client says, *I'm so frustrated with my current website company. My website has gone down three times in the last two months, and it costs me a bundle every time it does.* The eager professional replies, *That is unacceptable for your site to go down that many times. I would be happy to move your website over to my company and make sure that your site never goes down again. Would you want to do that?*

Whoa, back it up. Take a breath. Stay in the moment. You have more questions to ask. Don't be the doctor who asks two or three questions and then recommends that the patient have heart surgery in the morning.

The worst thing you can do is to sit in front of someone and tell him all the things that you and your company can do for him before you take the time to understand him. That behavior is condescending, insulting, and assuming.

Good questions make the process feel informal and pleasant for your buyer to talk. The more people talk, the more you'll learn about them. The more you know about someone, the easier it will be for you to help her make the right buying decision for her. Do what children do, and be curious. Ask away. You can't fake curiosity and sincerity.

Questions help you stay on target. They build credibility. Questions help you gain clarity. They enable you to diagnose problems prior to prescribing solutions. Doctors, police detectives, interrogators, and members of the military study this skill. They know that the right questions at the right time help them gain the clarity they need to pursue the correct solution.

Asking questions takes you out of your head and stops you from worrying about what you need to do or say. You remain in the moment asking questions and listening to the answers. It's not about having the perfect comeback or a snippy answer.

Asking questions in a completely random fashion is unproductive, unprofessional, and ineffective. Instead, questions should be used to pique the customer's interest and establish credibility in the initial meeting. Questions help you to identify the prospect's needs and uncover more accurate information from potential customers.

How you phrase and position your questions has a major impact on your customer's responsiveness. The right questions at the right time create the right opportunities. Avoiding the wrong questions makes room for the right ones.

I am often asked, *What happens if I forget a question? What do I do if I don't follow a list of questions that help me stay on track?*

People jump around in conversations. If someone says something pertinent to the conversation and you are not able to address it in the moment, make a mental note or write it down and re-visit the comment later.

Anytime you feel like you missed something important or you would like more detail about something that someone said, all you have to say is, *Do you mind if we re-wind our conversation a bit? Do you mind if we go back to something you stated earlier? I need a little clarity. Can we step back for a moment before we move forward? I need you to elaborate on something you shared before.*

The beauty of this type of conversation is that you follow a path, but the path is not set in stone. It becomes two human beings participating in a conversation, who move around from topic to topic, and it's fine to circle back and obtain more information. This allows you to chill out and stay present.

Over the years, a number of my clients have told me that they don't like the questioning part of the process. They don't like to feel uncomfortable and don't want to make others uncomfortable. I tell them that people don't make changes and don't have transformations in their lives when they're in their comfort zone and hanging out in the status quo. People change because they are not happy about where they are, or they're ready to make a change and say yes to a transformation.

If you think the way to keep your customers happy is by avoiding ruffling their feathers with tough, difficult questions, think again! Your clients can't solve their problems if they don't acknowledge them and discuss them. And that's where you come in. You help them to see the larger picture, the gravity of their situation, and what is possible.

It's tough love, in the form of questions that will help your clients recognize their problems. Asking tough, probing questions is major, but maybe you've been holding back from this because these questions may be imposing and intrusive. If you don't solicit more information, your potential client will find another professional who will, and that is your competition. Surface questions do not add value or make people think outside their comfort zone.

Most experts approach the questioning part of the process like a snorkeler. They ask surface questions, stay in the shallow part of the process, and never get to the real challenges that someone is facing. Some, however, are willing to go deeper, like a scuba diver, by asking pointed questions to uncover a few more layers about what is going on below the surface.

What is on the surface is never really what is going on.

Surface questions will never allow someone to open up to you and reveal the truth. If someone calls me and tells me that they want to close more sales in their client conversions or generate more profits in their business, that may be true, but through my questioning process we uncover the real reason why they want those results.

Through my inquiries, I find out that they're scared and stressed and on the verge of losing their home. Their spouse is complaining about how much money they're bringing in. They have ninety days to make something happen, or they will have to close their business. I could never get to the depth of their pain by staying on the surface.

Questions that delve into the prospect's life allow him to open up and tell you the truth. Your questions pinpoint his most pressing priorities and problems.

It's impossible to list all the questions that might come up as you're interacting with your prospective clients.

The following questions are designed to help you better understand your buyer's issues, current situation, convincing reason to change, and whether you are a good fit to help her at this time. Again, it sounds simple, and yet, loads of professionals are not going deep enough in their questions. You must go to the depths that reveal the truth of why you are meeting with someone.

Before you go into any meeting, presentation, consultation, or meeting you will want to do some pre-work to set yourself up for success. You have some questions to ask yourself.

Listed below are some questions to help you prepare for the meeting.

1. Have I determined the client's needs and expectations for this meeting?
2. What do I need to know about this person or company?
3. Who will be attending this meeting?
4. Does it make sense to have a brief telephone conversation with this prospect before my meeting?
5. What do I need to know about this client before I arrive?
6. Should I send this person information beforehand?

7. Have I let go of the *need* to produce any specific outcome and the need to secure the business?

8. Is my energy and intention in the right place?

9. Have I scheduled enough time to have a two-way dialogue?

10. What are three or four thought-provoking questions I can ask?

Use the questions below after you have prepped yourself and have obtained the prospect's preliminary information. (This is your question menu, listed in no particular order. Pick and choose which ones will work for you.)

- Can you share with me the reality of your current situation?
- Is there a specific reason why you wanted to meet with me today?
- Why has this issue not been addressed sooner?
- What would the consequence be of fixing this problem?
- What would the impact be of not addressing it?
- What has kept you from fixing this problem before now?
- Have you calculated the true cost of not taking care of this issue?
- Can you be more specific?
- What have you done to address the problem?
- How did this work or not work out for you?
- How did you feel about the way that things turned out?
- What else should I know about this situation?
- Could you give me an example?
- Can you be more specific about that?
- Could you give me some background information about what you just articulated?
- Can you please elaborate some more on that particular problem?
- What is the biggest challenge you have concerning that issue?
- How long have you lived with this problem?

- Could you expand on the challenge that you're having?
- Can you help me understand why that concerns you at this time?
- Could you describe for me what you consider to be the most serious problem you're facing right now?
- So that I may get a better sense of what's happening for you, can you tell me more about that particular challenge?
- Could you paint a picture for me about why this scenario keeps surfacing?
- Given the gravity of this issue, what do you think would be the most productive way to move forward?
- Can you describe for me what is worrying you about your current circumstances?
- Why is it essential that you find a resolution to this problem?
- Did this situation suddenly creep up on you, and when did you know that it was a problem?
- How long have you been dealing with this issue?
- Can you share more about what you just said?
- What are you doing right now to deal with this challenge?
- How have you tried to turn this problem around?
- What are you using or doing right now about this issue?
- Is doing nothing an option for you?
- What happens if you leave things the way they are?
- Where do you see this going if you don't take action?
- What would be the consequences to your health, your relationships, or your family if you stay with the status quo?
- What options or alternatives have you considered?
- What hasn't worked for you, and why do you think it didn't work?
- What is essential to you in finding a solution to this problem?
- Why are you seeking a solution now?
- Can you fix the problem yourself?

- On a scale of 1 to 10, where is your commitment level to change?
- Is anyone else involved in making this decision besides yourself?
- How soon would you like to move forward?
- Are you looking to get started sooner rather than later?
- When specifically would you like to get started?
- How has this issue affected your client satisfaction?
- How has this shaken your employees or business operations?
- How does this solution look/sound/feel to you?
- Is there anything that I have overlooked?
- Are there any final thoughts that you would like to share?
- How will you solve the problem if you don't engage someone to assist you?
- Have you thought through a budget for this project?
- How do you normally get approval for consulting of this nature?
- Who else will be involved in approving the budget?
- Can you walk me through the steps you need to follow to get funding for a program like this?
- A project of this kind ranges from $XXX to $YYY. How does that compare to what you thought it would cost?

These questions can get you started and can be a launch pad for your own personalized questions.

Use the questions judiciously. Ask the questions that are appropriate for your particular consultations. To be effective at using questions, you must be thoughtful, sensitive, and courageous.

I always ask the same question at the end of every meeting or consultation. Here is one of the ways I phrase this question. *Doug, before we wrap up, are there any lingering issues or additional concerns swimming around in your mind that we should talk about while I am here? It's helpful to make sure that we are both on the same page at this point. Then we can decide what the next best step is and where we should go from here.* Most of the time the buyer states that he thinks that we covered everything. I do not want to leave the meeting with some concern still in the room. I ask!

I want to leave every meeting on the same page as my potential client. We are in sync, and we are both crystal clear about the next step. Whatever that next step is, there are no surprises.

Everyone has a unique business, and everyone has a unique set of questions. This is where your expertise in your industry comes in. You know the types of issues that your clients have, build your questions around them.

Ask authentic and enlightened questions that add value in the consultation process and that move you closer to a better understanding of your client's issues and challenges. Then, weave in your perspectives and points of view about how you can help. The questioning phase of a consultation is a blend of advocacy and inquiry.

Questioner Beware: Make sure that your questions don't box people in or paint someone into a corner.

Do not propel yourself back to 1982 by asking these kinds of questions:

- Is there any reason why you and I can't start doing business together right this minute?
- What will it take to earn your business?
- Is there anything standing in the way to keep us from doing business today?
- If I can show you a way to save money on that widget, would you do business with me today?
- If I can get that price for you, are you willing to sign the paperwork now?
- Would you be in a position to do business with me today?
- How about we meet next week? How is Thursday at 2:00 p.m.?

The worst offenders are questions where there is only one answer. Your attempt to get someone to say YES by asking a question where YES is the only choice is dated and lame. Stop this or any version of this kind of trickery immediately:

- You do like to save money, don't you?
- You are looking to lower your monthly payment, right?
- You do think that saving for retirement is a wise idea, don't you?
- Don't you agree that having life insurance is an intelligent investment?
- You did say that you wanted to lose that baby weight, right?

And the prospect is thinking, *Do you think I'm foolish enough to fall for that crap because you tricked me by asking a question where the only answer is YES? I am way too shrewd for that B.S.*

Your role is to open up a conversation with someone. Your inquiries reflect curiosity and a genuine inclination to fully understand your potential client.

Chapter 21

Handling Objections

How you view and handle objections may have a significant impact on the outcome of your conversation. You can't work around objections, ignore them, or pretend that they are not there. A obstacle exists between you and your prospect, and it must be dismantled. Be mindful of this. Recognize your tendency to feel defensive, and replace it with empathy and curiosity.

During your consultations, it is common that some sort of objection will come up. How you handle the objection, not overcome it, may make or break what happens next.

Why do you hear objections? What do they mean? From here on out, learn to treat objections as if a prospect is saying, *I am not sold on the details that you've presented so far. Could you please give me more information so that I might make an educated decision?*

Your prospect needs more from you so that he may say yes with confidence. This is not the time to go old-school and try to overcome the objection. No one, I repeat, no one wants to be overcome. Buyers want to be heard, and they want you to treat their objections as real concerns.

Objections that you'll come across include: *Your fees are too high. It is not in the budget. I am going to think this over. This is going to be too hard to accomplish. Now is not the right time. There is too much on my plate right now. Our committee would like to wait. I need to check with my spouse.* Some of these objections are more common than others in your particular industry, but these are the ones that my clients talk about the most.

People often ask me what they should do or say when a prospect raises an objection. But that's the wrong question to ask. What you should be wondering is, *How do I avoid hearing objections in the first place?* Once you've heard one of these objections, you're already in trouble and have some work to do. Your buyers are telling you that you haven't shown them enough value to justify their investing in your offering.

If you always seem to be blasted with objections, you are probably making the classic selling blunder of telling more than asking, of talking more than listening. If you've asked penetrating questions and qualified your potential clients, you won't get many objections. For example, if you have an open and honest discussion about the cost of the investment, your fees for your service, you're not likely to hear the, *It's too expensive* objection. If you ask questions about the prospect's willingness to do the work necessary to fix her issue, you should not hear, *Now is not the right time.* And if you ask meaningful questions about her decision-making process and timeframe for making a decision, you won't hear, *I need to think about it.*

When a prospect poses an objection, acknowledge it, diffuse it, and address his concerns related to the objection. Understand what the client means. When you do, your conversations will remain gratifying and authentic, which is what prospects always want in the end.

When a potential client voices an objection of any kind, most of the time she is telling you that she is interested but that something is standing in the way of her saying yes. Objections may arise from a client who wants her doubts clarified, or she needs further information or reassurance about certain points. People don't ask questions and have objections unless they are seriously considering you and your service.

View the objection as a request for more information or as a prospect's concern or fear.

When a client states a concern, never interrupt him to attempt to overcome the objection. The more he talks, the more comfortable he will feel with you, and the more you will learn about concerns that he has. Make it a point to never disagree, because that will alienate the client by proving that you think he is wrong. You may win the war of words, but you will lose the business.

Show your client that you have no intention of becoming defensive or argumentative and that you are not going to try to overcome the objection that she has voiced. She needs to know that you heard her and that it's safe to be open and honest to share her concerns.

The last thing you want to do to someone when hearing an objection is to confront him with a slick expression or a quick comeback. That only serves to annoy him and perhaps even cause him to come up with more rational reasons for not buying.

You don't want a prospect to feel like you are going to accelerate the process, turn up the heat, sell her harder, and convince her to buy. This is the exact opposite of what you should be doing. There is never a need to jam, shove, or coerce someone to buy from you.

Your potential clients will not tell you when they're feeling the pressure, when they're uncomfortable, and they will not tell you that you are moving too fast. No one will come out and say, *Sally, I'm sensing you pushing me a bit hard, so I am pushing back because you're making me feel uncomfortable. Derek, I'm feeling a tad nervous right now because I've had some horrific experiences with salespeople in the past, and I don't like your approach. Janice, I need you to take a step back because I feel like this is more about you than it is about me.*

Prospects use their own language and will tell you that they need to think it over, that they have no money, or to call them in a few weeks. Most of the time, your potential clients aren't objecting to what you're selling but to how you're selling it and engaging with them.

When you hear objections that you suspect aren't real, that is an indication that your potential client has started feeling skeptical and distrustful.

Objections are a defense mechanism that potential clients use to protect themselves from people who are on a mission to close the sale at all costs. The responsibility is on you to help your potential clients overcome their suspicions of you.

Objections come in all shapes and sizes. If you keep yourself centered and calm you may diffuse the objection and re-direct the conversation. This in turn allows you to help your potential clients to be truthful about their situation so that they don't feel threatened. They need to feel sure that if they make themselves vulnerable with you, you won't take advantage of the information they share and try hard to sell them on your solution.

Let's use the example objection, *It is too expensive.* You could say:

- Tony, you have a legitimate concern regarding my fees. Here's what I am thinking. Let me know if this solution would work for you.
- Joan, let's talk about that, it sounds like we need to re-address the financial part of the proposal.
- Angela, it sounds like we may need to step back and discuss some payment options.
- Peter, I know that my fees might sound high, but I don't want to convince you why I am worth more than someone else. Do you mind sharing what is causing you to perceive this service as expensive?
- Thanks for telling me that, Alan, it seems like we should talk about that issue in more detail.
- Susan, what seems to be troubling you regarding my fees?

- Jonathan, I appreciate your honesty. Should we spend some time talking about that?
- Darlene, maybe we should take a step back before we move forward. Let's discuss my fee structure.

Listen and validate whatever the other person said to you without creating any resistance that might trigger hesitation and suspicion that suggest that you have a hidden agenda.

This immediately diffuses any pressure or tension that might be at the root of the objection and allows you to continue the conversation. I call it neutralizing the objection. You don't have to fight, overcome, or confront the objection. You neutralize it and deal with it by talking about it as opposed to shooting off a absurd remark, such as, *You do like quality, don't you? Are you looking for someone who is cheap or someone who does a great job? You can buy quality or you can buy garbage, pick one?* A biting retort makes people feel unheard, dismissed, and causes the walls to go back up.

The objection phase is a process, not a well-rehearsed script that you memorize every time you hear a particular objection.

Keep in mind that when you hear objections that you suspect aren't true, they're just a signal to you that your potential client is feeling hesitant, skeptical, or guarded. And because this concept of selling, of the stereotypical salesperson, is still so widespread, the responsibility falls on you to help your potential clients overcome their suspicion of you.

Responding with canned replies from the 1980's school of selling will cause the prospect to shut you down with no chance to re-open the conversation. You potential customer knows that you have a response for anything that he throws at you. He knows that you have a comeback waiting in the wings, ready to be fired off when necessary. Buyers know this because these responses have been used on them many times in the past.

We have all had these kinds of comebacks thrown in our face, and it never feels good. This is not the time to reach into a bag of tricks and pull out a generic song and dance routine that will make the client feel like her objection is not worthy of a genuine answer. This only makes you look like you stepped back in time, back into a style of overcoming objections popular decades ago.

From here on out you have other options, a different approach, and you will never fear an objection again. You can react to objections by dissolving pressure and creating a conversation based on trust so that both you and your client may collaborate about where to go next and whether you are a fit.

So, the next time you hear an objection, say to yourself, *Okay, there's an objection. I need to diffuse any pressure or tension that may be hidden beneath the surface, and I need to be sensitive to any resistance that my potential client may be feeling.*

Objections such as *I have no money and need to think about it* typically pop up because you may have not done an effective job in the previous parts of the consultation, or you skipped over the asking of probing questions, finding out about a timeline, discussing budget, and honing in on your value. If you speak about budget and fees early in the conversation, you will lessen the likelihood or eliminate the possibility of hearing the money objection. It should have been discussed already.

Some people get so bogged down in tricks, techniques, and having the right rebuttal to every objection that they don't use their natural skills for expressing empathy, asking questions, listening, and staying in the moment.

Objections are part of sales and business. But objections are nothing to fear or elude. Once you realize the underlying concerns that are behind most objections, it's much easier to diffuse, discuss, and turn them into positive buying decisions.

Let's face it. Buying can be a scary step. People will have legitimate concerns. It is an important part of your job to help prospects work through these fears and concerns. Your job isn't to overcome objections. Your job is to help your client be strong, be clear, and stay focused so that he can do what's right for him.

A Few Examples

Client Objection: *I would really like to work with you, but your fees are much higher than the two other interior designers with whom I have met.*

Typical Old-School Response: *Well, they are both good designers, but neither one of them specializes in XYZ. Neither of them is an expert who has a solution to your current problem. My fees are worth it because I have been in business for thirty years, and I will provide you with excellent this and spectacular that...*

So what! Whatever! All of this sounds to the prospective client like a mammoth justification, not an urgent reason why your fees are higher. It is your job to get underneath the objection and gain a better understanding of the client's objection.

My Suggested Response: *I appreciate you telling me that I'm your top choice and that you would like to hire me. However, it sounds like my higher fees are a stumbling block and that you would like to discuss them further? Is that correct?*

Let's take a step back and re-visit some of the specialized services that you are looking for and how I deliver them. Then we can talk about how those fees specifically work in the overall plan. How does that sound?

Next time you hear an objection, don't panic and think that you have to fight back and go into justification mode. Go into problem-solver mode instead. Below are three steps that you may use to handle any objection:

1. Call out the objection. Acknowledge its existence.
2. Probe a bit more for clarity. Ask a question.
3. Provide additional relevant information. Answer.

Acknowledge. *I hear what you are saying. That's not a problem. I understand that the timing is your biggest barrier. I appreciate you telling me that this has to go to the board for approval. It sounds like this is something that we should discuss a bit more. It seems like something we should address now, not later. Maybe we need to take a step back before we move forward.*

Ask. *Would you help me understand? Could you walk me through your concern just to be sure I understand? It sounds like you've been through this before. Can you tell me why you feel that way regarding the timeline?*

Answer. Insert your answer here.

Take these three steps: Acknowledge, Ask, Answer. Poof, objection handled!

This immediately reduces any pressure or tension that might be at the root of the objection and allows you to continue the consultation.

Whether the objection you hear is a kneejerk reaction, a genuine expression of concern, a smokescreen, a decoy, or a ploy, it's up to you to find out what the prospect means. If you can find out what the customer means, you may move forward. An objection means that there is an enormous boulder in the way and that it needs to be moved out of the way so that you may proceed. Remember, you can't work around it, disregard it, or pretend that it's not there. A barrier exists between you and the client, and together you need to move it out of the way.

Don't let hearing objections frustrate you. Be aware of and recognize a tendency to feel defensive, and replace it with empathy and curiosity. I've worked with people who try to escape, deflect, or sidestep objections all together. Other people hear objections and sell harder and push more. Some even become adversarial and hostile when hit with objections or what they perceive as objections. Understanding objections and confronting them head-on is the only way to deal with them.

Think of an objection as hitting the pause button. People pull out objections because they aren't sure what you might do or what you will say if they show their vulnerability.

Because a prospect is feeling vulnerable, this is the time to be gentle rather than pushy, to be tender instead of salesy.

This is the time to have compassion, not to view the prospect as just another sale.

If you pressure a potential client, he will stop trusting you, and you will lose the sale. But if he makes himself vulnerable by expressing objections and you listen and don't attack, he relaxes, remains open, and feels safe. And you may move forward without a hitch or hindrance.

In fact, unless I am working one-on-one with someone, I don't spend much time talking about how to handle objections and doling out advice about ways to get around them and what you say to overcome them.

The bigger issue is what you are doing to cause the objection. What is triggering the objection? Plenty of people don't bother to focus on why they're hearing objections in the first place. They would prefer to have a fast comeback and overcome the objection rather than to stop doing what is creating it initially. You now have a more constructive way to handle objections.

You will have to deal with objections. That's reality. The good news is that objections tell you exactly where to take the conversation next. So, if the customer says that she wants a discount, you clearly have to re-visit the value. Do not just give her a discount. If she says that she needs to think about it, re-visit the benefits and the timeline, do not just let her leave your office to think about it.

You feel more present, confident, and at ease when you know how to handle objections. With these tips, you'll find yourself less focused on memorizing the right thing to say at the right moment. You'll feel relaxed and spontaneous, as you find yourself much more aware of the flow of conversation and making sure that your potential clients feel comfortable with you.

Chapter 22

Fear Of The Money Conversation

Some professionals get squirmy when they have to talk to their clients about money. Talking about fees with clients is likely not on your list of favorite things to do. Few people like asking for money and talking about money. More than three-quarters of my clients face resistance or fear related to talking about money, price, or fees. I tell them that discussing money needs to be like breathing. It has to happen without you thinking about it. Money needs to be a straightforward element of every conversation.

Scores of us grow up hearing that money is one of a select smattering of topics, such as politics, sex, and religion, that should be avoided. You shouldn't brag about your net worth. You don't disclose your salary to colleagues. You don't ask friends about their income, mortgage, or money situation.

Since we have been discouraged from talking about money at every turn, it is no wonder that so many professionals sidestep the money conversation and become tongue-tied when necessity demands that they speak about it.

I was raised to view talking about money as a negative thing, taught that it was more risky than religion or politics and more vulgar than sex. Stay away from discussing money.

When I was eight years old, I asked my dad how much money he made...at Thanksgiving dinner with family and friends. His eyes almost popped out of his head, and he glared at me like he had seen a ghost. He stated, *That is none of your business, young lady, and it's impolite to ask anyone that that question. Don't you ever do that again.*

My past money messaging came back to haunt me decades later. I realized this when I considered how following my dad's advice had hurt me in my first sales job. When the money conversation came up for me, I choked. I stumbled over my words, and my hands shook. My belief about talking about money was no longer serving me, and I needed to do something about it. I had to be able to discuss money with clarity and confidence. I am pleased to share that I no longer suffer that particular penchant for self-sabotage.

If you are apprehensive because of your hidden money messages, you will wind up communicating your beliefs to your prospect. Here this loud and clear. What your prospect observes regarding your discomfort won't automatically be associated with your distress about money from your childhood messages. He will interpret your uneasiness as a lack of certainty in you and your products or services.

If any aspect of selling makes you squeamish, you may subconsciously try to escape doing it or only do it to the point of comfort. All human beings do this.

Mastery of any process requires you to be as conscious as you can about what you are doing. The greater the consciousness, the greater the mastery. You must face the fear, not turn away from it.

When it comes to talking about fees or money, many of the actions and behaviors that you were taught when you were younger become counter-intuitive. Messages like *Don't talk to strangers* and *Never talk about money* may linger in the back of your unconscious mind. You must make a deliberate effort to accept that your behavior needs to change if you wish to build your book of business. You must re-program your past perceptions of what is, and is not, acceptable in a sales environment.

Failure to have the money conversation with a prospective client raises doubts in the client's mind. To her, it's not logical and raises suspicion when you avoid the money conversation. When you avoid discussing money, you fail to set the ground rules on how and when you are going to get paid.

Reluctance to discuss fees at the beginning of a relationship may lead to awkward money conversations down the road. This includes the strained money conversation wherein you have to inquire, remind, and nudge clients to pay you. Get used to bounced checks, delayed payments, and sob stories, all because you resisted having a straightforward money conversation out of the gate.

Rarely do clients come out and tell you when you did something that caused them to take their business elsewhere.

Shelly, a CPA, called me after realizing her precarious position. *I need your help. I become inept when I talk about my fees and how I am paid. If I don't address this issue now, I will continue to lose business.*

Shelly informed me that a prospective client had come right out and told her that she perceived her clumsiness when talking about her fees.

The prospect stated, *If you are uneasy discussing your fees, I know that I will be uneasy about you handling my money.*

I know that talking about fees may be delicate, but there is no way around it. Part of my coaching work is to help my clients fashion their own unique and strategic money-talk for their business. I teach them to discuss their fees and explain how they are paid in a way that puts them and their client at ease. I show them how to clarify how their fees are paid, how the money will be used, and what happens when invoices are outstanding. This conversation is fair, firm, and productive.

You look clients in the eye and tell them, strong and straight, with confidence and clarity, *Helen, here are the details about how I am paid for my work. Jeremy, I would like to explain how I am compensated for the work that I do for you. Natalie, let's revisit the details of the payment process and how the money will be collected. Jack, let's discuss the payment options and how the money will be used. Anne, one of the conditions attached to my service is that I get paid on time and in full. I never want to have to chase you for payment because that becomes awkward for both of us. It is easier if we can agree on that now.* When you position the money-talk as a candid and straightforward conversation, no misunderstanding occurs about your fees and how you are compensated for your time and endeavors.

Here is an example of what a strong money conversation sounds like from my world. *Sarah, now that we've agreed to work together, let's align our expectations of each other as it relates to the program and how invoicing works. It's nice to get this out of the way so that you and I can start on the same page and stay there throughout our time together. I collect the first of four payments seven days prior to our first working session and the remaining three payments follow every thirty days. I want to be your coach and not a money manager, and I never want to put us in a situation where I have to remind you or chase you for payment. Marie, my assistant, will send you a monthly invoice. Is this a commitment that you can keep?*

This mutual and respectful money dialogue defines how you and your client are going treat each other and how the two of you will always be aligned. It relieves all the pressure concerning money and expectations.

You must personalize and customize a money-talk that matches your personality. I enjoy teaching professionals how to craft their customized language related to money and to do this in a way that is appropriate for them and that stirs a positive response in the client.

One of the strategies that I teach in my consulting practice is what I call *prepping the money conversation.*

You take the initiative to start the money or fee discussion with your clients at the beginning of a meeting, consultation, or conversation by dropping the money hint.

It shows that you are willing to open the door to talking about the subject of money. It is always better to raise the topic yourself and control the conversation than to potentially find yourself on the defensive or unprepared if a client says, *So, should we talk about money?*

Opening the door yourself helps normalize the discussion of money. At some point at the beginning of the conversation, you can say, *Joseph, I appreciate you coming in to meet with me today to discuss the details of your situation. I'd like to focus the first part of our conversation on the background of your unique circumstances and get some history regarding your current challenges. Then we can talk about how I work and the services that I offer to someone in your situation. Finally, if you feel like you are ready to move forward or begin the process, we can talk about the investment involved.*

You bring it up early and pave the way for the money conversation later. And when it is time to talk fees and discuss money you only have to say, *Now, let's address the fees involved.*

You want to arrive at a clear and mutual money understanding. Get the client to agree out loud. *Sally, does that make sense? Tom, do you have any questions about that? Beverly, is that clear to you?* Assure the prospect that everything you are communicating will also be in writing in an agreement or contract.

Prepping the conversation means that there are no surprises and no discomfort. You paved the way to step into the money conversation with confidence and strength.

When you drop the resistance and lose the fear related to talking about money, something miraculous happens. You get paid for your work. Shocking, right? Clients appreciate and respect experts who take a professional approach to the money discussion. Smart professionals know that stepping into a strong money conversation sets them up for advancement.

If you feel like you are chasing money, this means that your clients are dragging out payments, invoices are outstanding, and you are working for a client who is not paying you. Hop off of the hamster wheel! Fix this issue without delay. This open money wound will never heal itself.

I often listen to professionals blame their clients for unpaid invoices. They are shocked when a client does not bring his account current for sixty to ninety days, or even longer. They get upset that they are doing the work and feel that their clients are being disrespectful. They play the victim rather than the victor.

I tell these people that they set themselves up for this scenario every time they deliver a wishy-washy, half-hearted, and weak-willed money discussion. They are responsible for the client's behavior because they voluntarily evaded the money conversation.

Non-payment will continue until you step into the money-talk with poise. Eliminating the fear of the money-talk won't happen overnight, but in time, with persistence and perseverance, it will happen for you too.

Discussing fees and money involves more than words. It requires a shift in your money mindset, how you think and what you believe about money. There is no better time to fashion a new and happy relationship with money.

Chapter 23

Asking For And Closing The Business

At this point, you have uncovered your client's goals, issues, and obstacles. You have elaborated your thoughts regarding how you would address those concerns. You have discussed fees and handled objections. You have mutually removed all hindrances to moving forward into a new client relationship. The client has indicated her agreement to work with your proposed products or solutions. You are moving the consultation to its natural and logical next step: closing the business.

If there is one thing that has cost millions of people billions in revenue, it's the fear of asking for the sale. Asking for and closing the business is the most circumvented component of the sales process, and the most daunting. Professionals know that they have to ask, but the fear stops them dead in their tracks. They know better but often skip this step because of how it makes them feel. They're so consumed with how they feel when they must ask for the sale and gain a commitment that they don't consider how the prospect feels.

In the words of my dad, *If you don't ask, you won't get.* Prospective clients can't agree to work with you if you never ask the question. Not asking for the sale, especially if someone is a good prospect, is awkward. Think about how confused your client feels when you take up all of his time, discuss what you can do for him, share information about your services, and then don't bother to ask him for the business. While you're busy thinking about yourself and how anxious you are, you never give a thought to how tense your client feels.

The client is expecting you (if it's the right fit) to ask for the sale. Not making an attempt to close, or asking for the business, may cause the client to doubt you or your services. You send a silent message that indicates that you might not be the strongest and best choice.

If clients read nervousness in your body language, you won't close the sale. If you don't get comfortable and confident asking for the business, you better get comfortable with prospects going to your competition.

If you don't ask, the answer is always no. It is your job to ask for the business! Prospects don't always let you know what's on their mind. *Sounds good, let's get started. I'm sold, I want to hire you right now. I am ready, let's fill out the paperwork. Perfect, can we begin right away?*

Some experts are afraid of being perceived as the stereotypical salesperson so commonly seen as brash, insistent, and obnoxious. They do anything they can to not be portrayed in that light. Even though the person they are speaking with is their ideal client, they zip their lips and don't ask for the business.

Because of a subconscious fear of being perceived as that cliché salesperson, all too often people don't attempt to close the business. Or, if they do try to close the sale, they do not execute in a strong, assertive manner. Such women may come across as wishy-washy. You must ask for the business, or you won't have a business. You may do everything else right, prospecting, presentation, needs analysis, discussing fees, and handling objections, but if you don't close with proficiency, there's no sale.

It may help a bit to think of it this way. Most people need you to help them in the decision-making process. You are the one to move them to a decision. Whether it is a yes or a no or a next month or next year, prospects need you to nudge them in a way that causes them to take action in one direction or another.

Don't think of closing as pushing the prospect into doing something that she doesn't want to do. Instead, think of it as nudging her just enough to move her out of her inertia and into taking some kind of action.

If the fit is there, and you can see yourself as the right service provider for this client, not closing the sale is a disservice to him. You might as well stop the meeting and drive the prospect over to your competitor's office so that this person can finish the job for you. You are preventing the prospect from taking advantage of the benefits of your product or service.

If you think that selling or closing is unethical or distasteful, you must let that go. Delete from your mind the stereotypical perceptions of a closer and what it means to close the sale. Don't think that you need to be hostile, forceful, or offensive. If you feel that you must be over-zealous or objectionable, your approach needs a shift. Good closing skills have nothing to do with hard-hitting rhetoric or well-rehearsed one-liners.

Many closing strategies have been around for decades. These strategies either no longer work like they used to or may rub prospects the wrong way. Wise prospective clients have heard them all.

Closing is easy when you have one or two unique closes of your own. Find language that you are most comfortable with that reflects your personality and style so that you may win the business.

The only thing left to do is close the sale. Stalling, resisting, fearing, and attempting to shy away from this step will guarantee another lost sale.

Unless you complete this step you didn't score, you didn't complete the process. It's no different than taking all day to prepare a delectable meal, laying it out on the table, and then not eating it. It is no different than running a marathon and stopping a few yards shy of the finish line. You are not done.

All you are doing when you ask for the sale is giving your client a gentle tap in the direction of a decision. You never have to put him in a headlock, paint him into a corner, or tackle him to the ground to make a decision. You are asking him another question.

Closing starts the moment that the consultation commences, the moment that the conversation begins. The best and most undeniable way to close more business is to recognize that closing starts at the beginning. The most important skill isn't closing, it's opening. The opening is the new closing.

Most professionals who don't close the business ask themselves, *What happened at the end that caused the sale to fall through?* They're asking themselves the wrong question. They should be asking, *What did I do at the beginning of the consultation that might have caused an abrupt end to the possible sale?*

Making superficial adjustments and slight tweaks to the close will do nothing to increase profits. Fixing closing issues is like putting a Band-aid on a bullet would. If you learn to open the right way, the prospective client will likely close herself. She will ask you how to get started and what the next step is.

If the result of all of the hard work of attracting a prospect and meeting with him doesn't result in gaining a new client or winning more business, it means that something is broken, something is off that is causing a prospect not to feel comfortable hiring you. He can't see the value that you provide. If you are not closing the business, it's a blatant indication of a more costly problem.

Clients are rarely lost because you can't close effectively. No one will ever tell you, *Karen, you were my first choice, you are brilliant, and I would like to retain your services. Unfortunately, I can't. You're a rotten closer. Martin, I was hoping that you were going to be a more charismatic closer. I'm sorry, I won't work with an expert who can't seal the deal with zest.*

No! The close is a result of a well-managed and thorough execution of the entire initial client consultation process. It's a natural culmination of a superb conversation throughout the consultation.

The reason why fixing closing problems is unproductive is that the result is only superficial. What's left untouched, what is missed, what is overlooked are the underlying dynamics that perpetuate the problem. If you want more clients, better results, and improved profits, you must be willing to fix the entire process. If it is fixed once, the rewards may be reaped over and over.

Knowing a few principles or closing strategies is not enough. You need to know them cold. My clients role-play this with me from open to close, discussing money and overcoming objections. They own it. They use it to convert interested prospects into invested clients with authentic confidence.

Many professionals remark, *I don't want to force someone to work with me. I don't want to pressure someone.* What? Who said anything about forcing someone to hire you? If you have to use pressure, your approach is all wrong. Get help.

Other business owners indicate that they don't want anyone to think that they are selling something. Really? You're not fooling anyone pretending that you're not selling something. You are, and everyone knows it. It's time to drop the disguise and be the stand-out professional behind your remarkable services and expertise. You *are* selling yourself and your services.

Wishing, hoping, and praying for the sale is not nearly as lucrative as asking for the sale. One of the things that you can do at the end of the meeting or the end of the call after you have done all of the hard work is to maintain the momentum that you started in the process by setting up what I call the next steps. You have an obligation to ask your client for some commitment. Keep in mind that this looks different for each client.

Signals from the prospect may be covert or subtle. They may be direct or obvious verbal signals. *We would collaborate well with each other. This seems like an easy process!* These signals could also fall anywhere in between.

You're now at the next step, getting a yes, a no, or a maybe. There are countless ways to ask for the business. Getting to this point and stopping the momentum is going to have to be a thing of the past. It is not your client's job to indicate to you that he is ready to begin or is ready to work with you. It's your job to make something happen next. All you have to do is ask.

Below are a few examples of ways to ask for the business. This list should be a good starting point for you. If the meeting is going well, pull out your audacity and ask:

- What are your thoughts about proceeding in this matter?
- You mentioned that you need our service immediately. Does that mean that you would like to begin as soon as this week?
- Now that we've modified the proposal to your specifications, shall we move forward and begin the paperwork?
- Earlier you said that you'd like to have this in place by the end of the month. What do you suggest for our next move?
- When would you like to move forward and begin the process?
- Based on what we talked about, would you like me to prepare a detailed proposal?
- Based on what you shared with me, it seems like a good fit. What do you think about retaining me to represent you?
- Now that you know more about my services and how we would work together, are you comfortable moving forward?

Asking for the business using a fresh and modern approach like the above is more profitable for you and feels better for the client. It is up to you to discover ways to ask that best fit your style. If you have the solution to your prospect's problem, all you have to do is say so. Ask when you can get started, so all that's left to do is work out the details.

It's your job to close and to find a way to do it that feels right for you. All parties involved should know what is going to happen next. Moving forward with complete clarity on both sides, making sure that everyone is on the same page, is an efficient way to do business.

I see too many people get to this point in the process, and they ask for the business, but they use passive and pathetic closes. I have heard professionals close by using language such as, *Well, why don't you let me know when you want to get started. How about you give me a call when you're ready? Please keep me posted as to when the time is right for you.*

This language may sound like a close, but it is not. It is weak and half-hearted. It is up to you to ask for the sale. By changing the way that you ask for the business, you will automatically increase your closing percentage.

Chapter 24

Follow Up And Follow Through

Following up is one of my favorite topics! Unfortunately, not many business owners feel the same way. Here is my shot to demonstrate the importance of adding this dynamic art to your business arsenal. Following up is rudimentary and so easy to accomplish. Please note that we have another F word here.

Why would someone bother to start a business, deliver a presentation, meet with a new client, and then not take the time to follow up? How in the world can you not find the time to follow through and complete the transaction that you've started? If you willingly let your customers fall through the cracks due to a lack of organization or poor communication, you will jeopardize the sale and your professional reputation, and the potential for referrals will vanish.

Not following up is an epidemic, and this form of self-sabotage is within your control. If you ever utter the words, *I forgot, I ran out of time,* or *I will follow up tomorrow,* you're pressing down hard on the brakes of your business. Not following up is one of the reasons why businesses fail.

Let's be honest, you didn't forget to call someone back, you didn't run out of time, you didn't happen to get sidetracked. You chose not to do what you needed to do. You made up a good excuse (a.k.a. the lie you tell yourself to make yourself feel better) and let yourself off the hook. You fully participated in forgetting, running out of time, and getting sidetracked.

I see this every day in my business and hear people default to making excuses over taking action. Either you or someone close to you conveniently forgot to do what they said they would do and then made up a good excuse why they forgot. There is no such thing as a good excuse, only a well thought out lie. That may have worked when you were 5-years-old, but you are now a grown-up businesswoman, and that behavior is no longer cute.

Sometimes things happen, and on a rare occasion, you do forget, but I am not talking about once in a blue moon, I'm talking about blatant ball-dropping and business neglect. I do realize that everyone is busy and that sometimes tasks fall through the cracks.

The habit of honoring your word and keeping your commitments costs nothing, but not keeping your word can cost tens of thousands of dollars! Come on, you're just following up, not climbing Mount Kilimanjaro. How hard can following up with someone be?

A Lost Art

Neglecting to finish what you've started shows a lack of commitment on your part to your potential customer. People who are serious about their business follow up and would never dream of dropping the ball on potential business. The question isn't how many sales you are making each week, it's how many sales you are losing each week. Sales follow-up is a critical part of selling, and omitting this crucial step creates a fatal flaw in your process. Dropping the ball at the follow-up stage sends a message to clients that they can't count on you. It is a reputation-destroyer. Is that the impression that you want to leave with your potential customers, that you talk the talk but don't walk the walk?

Think of a situation where you started a discussion with someone that you thought about doing business with. You took phone calls, participated in meetings, sent e-mails, and then got close to where you thought that they would follow up with you, but they never did. You got nothing! They fell off the map, as if your conversations never happened and meant nothing to them.

They left you surprised at their behavior and disappointed that you wasted your precious time. Why bother to begin the sales process when you have no intention of finishing it?

Think about the number of times that you, as a customer, have walked away from a business because of poor follow-up. How many times were you willing to pay more for a product because of perceived better service? Poor communication or lack of responsiveness is a leading reason why clients leave businesses for a competitor.

This appalling business behavior must stop! Following up is the easiest fix for most businesses, and it is an instant way to generate more sales. Following up is within your control, it's your choice, and it's an easy way to differentiate yourself from other professionals who are neglecting to follow up.

Avoid The Dreaded *Just Following Up* E-Mails

Stop pestering and start profiting. Do you want to differentiate yourself, stand out, and rise above the noise? One easy and surefire way to do this that will put you miles ahead of the other professionals in your industry is in your follow-up approach and the language that you choose.

The same over-used, ineffective, outdated, and irritating follow-up messages waste your prospect's time and trigger a negative response in him. Does this sound familiar? *Hi Mack, I wanted to follow up and see if you have any questions regarding the proposal I sent? Hi Samantha, I wanted to reach out again since I haven't heard from you. Hi Thomas, I want to check in one more time to make sure that you have what you need in terms of information regarding the workshop. Hey Justin, I'm touching base to see if you're still interested in working together? Hi Danielle, I'm following up after our meeting last week. Hi Ethan, I wanted to reach out to see if you are still interested in working together? Hey Gregg, I was just checking in to see if you got my last eleven e-mails?*

Stop this lunacy! This type of lazy language follow-up fails because it adds no value to anything. All you do is create the kinds of empty or annoying messages that prompt people to disengage with you. It is the fastest way to the delete button. Launching into such boring vanilla messages will deliver feeble results. Weak follow-up e-mails result in nothing more than client aggravation and irritation.

Just following up, checking in, reaching out, or touching base e-mails may make you feel like you are moving a prospect forward, but you're not. They may make you feel like you are keeping the momentum going, but you're not. They may make you think that you are doing something productive, but the effort is hollow and meaningless. Plus, billions of other people are using the exact same language. They are just following up, just reaching out, just checking in, and just touching base too. Talk about ordinary and monotonous. You are blending in versus standing out.

Leave out the words *I was just following up, checking in, reaching out, or touching base*. I challenge you to write e-mails or leave voicemails that do not include this language. Doing this takes you off of auto-pilot and allows you to engage in a different and noticeable way.

E-mails that use the above language are annoying and disruptive to the recipient. They add no value whatsoever. If you are attempting to re-connect by using the same *just checking in* message, how can prospects differentiate you from anyone else in their inbox? Let's be clear. You do need to follow up. But you do not need to use the same sleepy language used by everyone else, and this includes the alarming, *Hi, I'm just following up...*

In today's super-busy, fast-paced world of constant intrusions, people are reading their e-mails with their finger on the delete button. You can't afford to interrupt prospects without providing some value and a compelling reason for them to keep the verbal exchange going. If you're not connecting with prospects, it's time to shake things up, rattle the cage, and change your language so that you may generate different results.

But before you change your language, ask yourself this, *Did I take the time to establish the rules of the follow-up with my prospect? Have I added value in all of my communication with this prospect? Did I ask my prospect when we will continue the conversation? Did we clearly discuss and define what the next steps would be? Did I ask how we will openly communicate moving forward?* Discussing the rules of communication will save you so much time and help your correspondence be viewed as a welcome e-mail or voicemail as opposed to being an annoyance.

You can radically change the way your prospects interact and stay in touch with you. Start saying, *The last time we spoke you mentioned X. Based on the deadline that we discussed, we need to do Y. In our last conversation, you suggested that I re-connect with you to talk about Z. Mike, I wanted to re-connect to see if you are open to continuing the conversation that we started in January? Marsha, when we talked, we seemed to be on the same page regarding moving forward.*

Get creative! Be different! When you change your approach, you will produce different results. When you change your language, you stand out and win more business.

Actions speak louder than words! It's time to stop talking about following up and engage instead in this income-generating task. You won't regret it.

Another Overused And Outdated Word Choice

Do you tap out daily e-mails using lazy language, or are you sending modern and dynamic digital mail to ensure that you are coming from a position of strength and confidence?

Everyone is overloaded with what feels like an endless stream of daily e-mails. Many have a similar theme and an outdated feel. They are self-serving and all about the sender. How many times a day do you send an e-mail with the words *love* or *I would love to* in them? *Love* has become a ubiquitous word used by professionals far too casually. Use of this word will cause the recipient of your e-mail to immediately dismiss your message. Stop irritating savvy clients by sending e-mails filled with the *love* language. *Love* and business don't mix.

Here is what it sounds like to barge into someone's inbox and drop the L bomb: *I would love to meet you for a cup of coffee. I would love to set up a meeting and tell you about my business. I would love to get together to tell you about our new products. I would love to work with you. I would love to schedule twenty minutes to show you a demo.*

Is the *love* word infecting your prospecting e-mails and business correspondence? Just because that is what you'd love to do, does that mean that it's something that the recipient of your e-mail also desires? You are telling the prospect what you love rather than asking her if she is interested in your product or service.

I challenge you to look at the last two dozen e-mails in which you sent a *love* note to a potential client. You probably infused some love into your e-mails and possibly even into your voicemail messages. You shared lots of love with your prospects. In doing this, you are blending in and being forgettable.

I have talked to dozens of business owners who have told me how much they hate the word *love*. When they see that word in e-mails or hear it in voicemails, it makes them to classify the sender as another self-serving professional looking to steal their precious time. They would *love* for you to stop this dreadful business practice and get lost. Move off of auto-pilot, be more creative. It's time to go from sending mindless messages to growing more conscious in your professional language.

Using the word *love* adds no value to your message, it fails to engage prospects, and it moves you no closer to getting what you want. E-mails filled with *love* will generate low interest and produce high resistance.

The Fix

I show professionals how to take the spotlight off of themselves and focus on a more collaborative approach. As much as I preach about this, some people refuse to stop using such lazy language. These are the same people who ask me why their calls and e-mails go unanswered.

I take people off of auto-pilot using self-centered *I* language and teach collaborative phrases such as:

- Are you open to having lunch to discuss X?
- Are you available to talk on the phone next week?
- What are your thoughts on sitting down to discuss Y?
- What do you think about syncing up our calendars to finish our conversation from last week?

By asking if someone is open to your request and using language that gives them some say, you set yourself up to have more of a dialogue rather than a monologue. Did you notice that I used the word YOU in each example? Appeals that make it all about yourself don't land well and cause people to resist your request and deem you to be self-serving. Make it about the other person, and you will never been seen as a self-absorbed professional.

I bet you do this too. Do you say things like, *I love your hair. I love your tie. I loved your presentation. I love your book. I love your blouse.* Instead of making the compliment about you, make it about the other person. Say instead, *Your hair looks nice today. Your tie looks great with that suit. Your presentation was super informative, I enjoyed it. Your book was thought-provoking. Your blouse is so beautiful and colorful.*

Do you see a theme here? Take yourself out of the equation. When you make the compliment about the other person, it feels genuine. Try this subtle and powerful language shift.

Go to a party, an event, a conference, or a networking meeting, and listen for how many people resort to lifeless *love* lingo. Stop spreading so much business *love,* and watch how people respond to you. Love is great! Love is good! Everyone loves some love. Love your family. Love your pets. Love the planet. But please, leave the *love* out of your business correspondence.

Watch for all over-used and outdated language in all of your written and spoken communication. This may be costing you sales and opportunities.

Chapter 25

Honesty Is Always In Style

Honesty can boost conversions, trust, and sales! Numerous potential customers cry out for transparency. When you tell the truth and give honest advice, you reap rewards and referrals. Today's buyers find truthfulness, clarity, and humility refreshing.

I believe that most professionals are honest. Of course, there are, and will always be, companies that hire people who are good at stretching or hiding the truth. Some people omit key details and say anything to close the sale. I am thankful that this is changing, and people who behave that way are fading away.

Honesty sells. Being truthful is a key component in boosting conversions and sales. Telling it like it is has some concrete advantages and perks. You engender better communication, build stronger relationships, and develop deeper levels of trust while you're selling if you're honest and transparent. Being honest means that you always find yourself in a win-win situation.

Lies and mistruths damage the ability of salespeople to communicate with their clients. They also result in a complete communication breakdown that is difficult or impossible to repair.

It amazes me how some salespeople stretch the truth, mislead the customer, misrepresent their company, product, or service, and omit information. While this will certainly work once or twice, most people seldom fall for this approach twice. In the long run, you might win the battle, but you will lose the war.

Below are five simple core concepts that will help you with honesty, if this is a challenge for you. These ideas originated from business owners with whom I spoke.

1. **Lose the *close-the-sale-at-all-costs* mentality.** Buyers can feel that negative energy coming at them. There are no winners with this one. If the fit is good and the situation is right, by all means close the sale. If not, walk away.
2. **Honor your words.** Do what you say you will do, when you say you will do it. If you make a promise to a client, keep it. If you tell someone that you will do something, make sure you follow through. This, more than anything else, will demonstrate that you are dependable and can be counted on.
3. **Be on time for your appointments.** Being late is an epidemic. Excuses for being late are endless. Showing up late and saying, *I'm sorry I'm late, traffic was terrible,* is probably stretching the truth. Be honest and say, *My apologies for being late. I didn't give myself enough time to get here.* Regardless of how long you have worked with a particular customer, make sure that you arrive on time for your meeting. If, for some unforeseen reason, you are going to be late, call. Your clients are busy too. Show them that you respect their time.
4. **Be authentic and drop the act.** How you behave and interact with your clients and customers should not be an act. Enough said!
5. **Never exaggerate what your product or service can do.** Discover the true benefits and value of your product or service, and communicate this in an effective way to your prospects. Make sure you do this in a manner that matters to the client.

These may sound like simple concepts. However, I guarantee that many of your competitors are not executing them on a regular basis. Everything you do influences the level of trust that you develop with your customers and prospects.

Some professionals get caught up in their own agenda. They forget to tell the truth. They fail to mention details that could make or break the value for a customer. You're better off telling the truth and losing the sale than you are lying or misleading the customer.

Honesty has always been and will forever be the best (sales) policy. You may or may not get the sale. But I would rather lose a sale than lose my integrity.

This chapter was short by intention because we all learned in kindergarten that honesty is the best policy. This is simply a brief reminder for those who may have forgotten this important lesson.

Chapter 26

The Downside Of Technology

Technology can be an exceptional asset to help you close more sales, if you know how to use it well. It may also be damaging if you don't. As a professional, have you become too dependent on technology to do your selling for you? Your business depends on how well you sell, not on how well you play with your technology.

There are plenty of good things about technology in the tools we use, but there is a human and emotional element that some specialists have forgotten about. Technology gives people the illusion that they are becoming more connected when, in reality, it's crippling their social skills. Liking, sharing, favoriting, and commenting on posts might seem like a sincere way to establish or maintain treasured relationships, but no amount of likes or thumbs-up buttons will replace genuine human interaction.

If you truly want to stand out and differentiate yourself, you need to step away from technology and step into real conversations. Stop typing and texting and start talking! Get back to what really works, a personal connection. People close sales. Technology doesn't. Technology will never compensate for a deficiency in your sales and communication skills.

Selling is, and always will be, about people collaborating and building solid business relationships. While your competition is wasting time typing endless e-mails to prospects and trying to generate appointments, schedule meetings, and close some business, you should be talking to your prospects voice-to-voice or on a virtual face-to-face platform, such as Skype or Zoom.

I am witness to the headaches of experts who are trying to convert interested clients and website visitors into paying clients. Buyers are showing up, but business owners fight to convert them into paying clients. Some people believe that increasing their presence and casting a wider net is the magic bullet necessary to increase revenue and close sales. Social media is part of a sales strategy, not the be all and end all of it.

Great sales and relationship skills turn website visitors into paying clients. All the social media in the world will not yield results if your potential customers are not buying what you're selling. When the critical skill of sales is left out of the social media equation, businesses fail.

Every day I listen to business owners tell me that they have no budget set aside for sales training. I hear instead that budgets have gone into a social media campaign. Some people are choosing to invest money into the passive part of the business. Now hear this. A social media strategy combined with updated sales skills work together, they do not work independently of each other.

If you're ready to start taking action to make the right kind of changes, try some of these smart sales practices:

- Commit to communication face-to-face, eye-to-eye. Do you want to make someone feel special? Pick up the phone, make an appointment, or schedule a video chat. Face-to-face or phone connections beat email correspondence every time. The phone is still the best weapon you have to secure a meeting.
- Use a more modern approach, and throw out the old procedures. While you need a roadmap and a game

plan, including practiced phrases, move away from the blandness of memorized scripts that sound like every other voicemail or e-mail your prospects receive. Proactive and productive conversations produce results, word-for-word scripts do not.

- Separate yourself. Stop following the masses. Just because someone says that social media is the quickest way to close sales and grow your business doesn't mean that it will work for you. Break away from the pack, and be yourself. Be willing to stop long enough to assess the best path to take toward your revenue goals.
- Take the right action. In my consulting work, I see a lot of professionals spending their days sending e-mail after e-mail, trying to connect with everyone and their mother on social media. They don't realize that they are adding to the clutter of their prospect's already overstuffed inbox. They're not willing to step out from behind the cloak of technology and into the messy world of personal relations. Do what we did back in the day. Talk to someone face-to-face. Risk people getting to know you.
- Mesh high-tech with high-touch efforts. I'm not suggesting that you drop your devices and your social media communications entirely. They do make a great foundation for your company's general message. Use them as the credibility that backs up what you say face-to-face. Remember that even the most engaging e-mail campaign is only meant to start a conversation. The real magic happens with that most important of sales ingredients, you. You are the most important tool in your toolbox.

I am all for technology making our businesses better, but where do we draw the line? I challenge you to step away from your computer and your tablet, and go build some genuine relationships. Use your phone to have a real conversation. Be that invaluable connection and memorable encounter that your customers crave.

Chapter 27

Relinquish Your Busy Badge

I don't have enough time. I am too busy. I can't do that right now. I am so swamped. I am crazy busy at this time. I can't add one more thing to my plate. Are you a member of the complain, whine, and moan club?

Those excuses are more common than the common cold. When life and work get busy, or when you don't want to feel guilty about avoiding a task or an obligation, the time excuse rolls off of your lips.

Stop convincing yourself that you don't have the time. Everyone is busy, and lamenting your lack of time means nothing to anyone. Chronic excuse-making is an excellent way to evade doing the work that needs to be done.

Since no one has figured out how to add more hours to the day, the best you can do is use the time that you do have more efficiently. No miracle tool exists that will eliminate the work that we all have to do on a daily basis.

You Cannot Manage Time

You can only manage your priorities. I don't believe that you have a time-management problem. You have a priority-management dilemma.

Jim Rohn says, *When you want to do something, you make the time. When you don't, you find an excuse.* How true. How many times a day or a week do you utter an income-killing phrase? Take ownership of the time you do have. Your time is your most valuable resource. Don't misuse it.

It's Time To Relinquish Your Busy Badge

Professionals who have the right attitude think: *Even though I'm busy, I will make time for prospecting this week. I will work a few extra hours and network on LinkedIn. I will attend a lunch meeting, even though my schedule is tight.*

We all have the same twenty-four hours in a day. You are either using your time prudently or frittering it away.

No one has enough time in the day for everything they want to do. However, if something is a priority, you must make the time. When you find yourself thinking, *I don't have time,* it may mean that that particular task is not a priority or that you didn't want to do it in the first place, so you blame it on time. But blaming time itself is nonsensical.

I believe that *I don't have time* is code for *I don't have the desire.*

Hundreds of books and thousands of articles dispensing advice about how to manage time are out there, but time-management skills are of no value if you don't know what things to manage or don't know what your priorities are.

Time is precious. Time is not your enemy. It is important to figure out what is the highest priority on the to-do list and what can wait. Ask yourself: *Is this urgent, important, or non-essential?* If you want something bad enough, nothing will stop you, nothing will get in your way. Even mountains will crumble into molehills.

Why would you want to broadcast to the world that your time-management skills are pathetic?

Things That You Might Be Saying ... Or Whining

- I'd like to get out of my office and network more, but I don't have time right now.

- It would be so nice to have coffee and re-connect, but I don't know where I would find the time.
- I should go to more conferences, but with my schedule, there's no time.
- I know I should leave my office more, but I am super busy.
- I've worked myself to the bone, and I'm too tired to make the time.

The list goes on, but the theme is the same. People blame time itself for all of their incompletions, inefficiencies, lack of production, and the absence of income and clients. Blaming time is an easy and socially acceptable excuse. Time is a concept that has no vested interest in what you do with it. Time never did anything to you. You cannot control much in life, but you can control the way that you spend your time.

The in-your-face reality is that blaming a lack of time for your failure to act usually means that you never wanted to put forth the energy to complete the task. As a result, professionals expend their time and energy justifying their lack of performance instead of focusing on ways to improve it. They are becoming adept at the *I-don't-have-time* excuse.

I am sympathetic to family and work commitments. But time accommodates the committed, those searching for the holy grail of achievement.

Everyone is busy. Life is busy. Even toddlers are busy. You are not the only person who is busy. You and I each have the same amount of time every day. Everyone on earth has one hundred and sixty-eight hours to divvy up throughout the week. It is what you do with your time that determines where your business ends up. Pay attention to how many times a day you blame a lack of time for not getting things done.

This distasteful ritual may be averted. Pay attention to how much time you squander every time you find yourself researching for hours on the Internet, scrolling through your Facebook page, or checking LinkedIn.

It does not matter the profession, you still need to keep up the pursuit. You must make time to keep your client pipeline full. Time is not your adversary.

Being responsible for how you use your time is the process of seeing it, owning it, solving it, controlling it, and doing it. Scrutinizing your use of time requires a level of ownership that includes doing what is necessary and focusing on proactive accountability, not reactive excuses.

Making excuses keeps you stuck in the same pattern of not being responsible for yourself and your business. Excuse-making is not the conduit to victory, surrendering your busy badge is.

Do you need to relinquish your busy badge?

Chapter 28

Carve Out Your Own Path

You are now at the point where you must make a decision. Will you make the commitment to implement what you have learned? Will you master the steps in the conversion process? Will you be one of the few professionals who make money, not excuses? Will you produce sales cake or sales crumbs?

Zig Zigler says, *If you're not willing to, no one can help you. If you're determined to, no one can stop you.*

Reading this book is not enough. Results come from the transfer of skills. To produce real improvement, you must make a commitment to apply new skills. You must make this process a part of who you are, every day, in every way. This takes a discipline and persistence that many people lack.

By committing to become a top producer, you take the step of implementing the strategies outlined in this book, and I have accomplished my goal in writing it.

One thing that stops people from taking a giant leap forward and creating momentum is that they don't know where to begin to gain some traction. They are overwhelmed with how to make sales work for them in their business.

I tell people that once they get the business bonfire started, it doesn't take tons of work to keep it going. I also share that the solution is easier and cheaper than staying with the status quo. This means that it is far less expensive to fix what is broken than it is to allow their practice to continue bleeding.

Building your business can be done by investing a limited amount of time each day. And yet most people don't do it, not regularly, anyway. They resist. They make excuses. Or they start something new, and in a few weeks they start something else. They promise themselves that they will begin next month or next year.

It's not like they dig their heels in and holler, *I think I'll run my business into the ground. Today I feel like driving my business off the road.* They don't have to speak those words because their actions demonstrate it all.

I understand. I fought that demon when I was building my business. Even when things were tough, and I had to make it work, I didn't do everything that I knew I should be doing. I admit it. I was scared. I was unsure of my next best move. I knew that I needed to ask for help, enlist someone to hold my hand, walk me through the process, talk me down from the ledge. You may need that too.

No one can compel you into action. No one can move your feet for you. You, and only you, can make the change and produce results. Don't waste another moment not taking action. Be responsible for your life.

Nothing in this book will work for you unless you make the bold choice to take action. Success will be impossible unless you add a massive dose of action.

Think about how many deals or how much money you lost this year because you didn't have a process that you could rely on over and over. Maybe tens of thousands.

You don't have time to figure everything out on your own. Plus, going solo is the most expensive way to grow a business. It costs you time, money, clients, and opportunities.

I see business owners misdiagnose themselves and wind up fixing their conversion issues with something that usually doesn't address the problem. They listen to others tell them what to do because something worked for someone else in their practice. They try to be everywhere doing everything. That never works, and you wind up pulling your hair out and screeching things like, *I'm not getting anywhere! I am tapped out, stressed out, and maxed out! I'm spinning plates and running in circles!*

These professionals have no clue what will work the best for their situation. When I work with someone who feels stuck, we start out with three or four easy, gratifying, and adroit strategies and then take them and run like hell. And then we build off of that.

If you want the future to be better than the present, you must make a move. To bust out of your current circumstances, you must have a goal and a purpose that is significant enough to prompt a change, a reason that is compelling enough to make it worth the discomfort of changing, and the discipline and drive to see it all the way through.

Ask yourself this. *Am I moving in the direction in which I wish to go? Are my actions aligned with my goals?* If not, you may do one of two things. You may commit to taking action, or you may lower your goals and expectations and do nothing.

The interesting thing about not doing anything is that you know exactly what tomorrow will look like, and the next day, and the next year, and the next decade. If you want security and certainty about the future, take a look at what you're committing to do today.

Those who thrive commit to taking action. They are all-in on every level. All-in means that there is no backing out. It means that there is no turning around. It's like deciding to dive into a pool. Once you decide to go all-in, you can't stop mid-air.

When you go all-in, you look at every activity. Every activity has a specific planned outcome. Your actions have a purpose, and that purpose produces results.

Become A Person Of Action!

Some people are doers and action-takers. Some people are born thinkers and are slow to take action. Some think about doing and never get anything done. There are many ways to become a person of action. You must know, without doubt, that taking action is the fastest, most efficient way to success. The evidence is compelling and obvious. Action produces results, inaction produces nothing. You must decide that doing nothing is no longer an option.

Action-oriented people are organized, persistent, energetic, and know exactly how to move from one project to another, effortlessly and without hesitation. Others flounder in a world of disorganization and inaction, jumping from one project to another and never working a project through to completion. At the end of the day, the doers have more energy than at the beginning of the day because they feed on taking action.

Andy Andrews offers this profound advice about action: *I am a person of action. I am energetic. I move quickly. Knowing that laziness is a sin, I will create a habit of lively behavior. I will walk with a spring in my step and a smile on my face. The lifeblood flowing through my veins is urging me upward and forward into activity and accomplishment. Wealth and prosperity hide from the sluggard, but rich rewards come to the person who moves quickly.* This quote hangs on the wall in my office to remind me of what is possible.

There comes a point at which you need to quit thinking, researching, planning, and talking, and just do something! It's time to conquer the fears, self-doubts, and insecurities related to selling.

It's not the best business idea that transforms a slow business into a booming business, it's the person who takes action and moves toward the launch who achieves victory. Action increases momentum, and momentum provides the ongoing catalyst to accelerate you to the next step, and the next step, and the next.

No one can force you into action. No one can move your feet for you. Only you may make the change and create the results. Don't waste another minute, day, or year not taking action in the direction in which you wish to go.

In additional insight from Andy Andrews, he writes: *I am a person of action. I am daring. I am courageous. Fear no longer has a place in my life. For too long, fear has outweighed my desire to make things better for my family. Never again! I have exposed fear as a vapor, an imposter that never had any power over me in the first place! I don't fear opinion, gossip, or idle chatter, for all are the same to me. I do not fear failure. For in my life, failure is a myth. Failure only exists for the person who quits.* Andy sums it up eloquently.

Making a change from where you are to where you want to go requires you to take action in that direction to generate momentum. Motivation gets you started, and habit keeps you going.

Every morning we get up and go through the day with habitual reactions to every situation. We operate on auto-pilot, the pre-conditioned patterns of our lives. We can, however, fashion positive habits in our lives. We can build new structures, unique patterns that produce greater abundance, joy, and happiness.

The law of inertia states that *a body at rest tends to remain at rest, and a body in motion tends to remain in motion.* Understand the power that even the tiniest of actions can have when taken in the direction of your goals, dreams, and desires. Just think what your business will look like in a week, next month, and a year from now.

The power to reach your goals lives within you. Remove the limitations that you have accepted, and you will be drawn to your goals and success as an anchor is drawn to the bottom of the ocean. Go sell without selling your soul.

Assistance From Liz

If you want help, maybe a little nudge, a gentle push, or a considerable shove, I'm your gal. Let me assist you in being bold and brave, committed and consistent, driven and decisive.

If you want to have a continuous stream of ideal clients and close more business, you must put some skin in the game and build a plan and a system that will serve you in this endeavor. I am here for you.

Let's start a conversation. E-mail me or call me if you have questions, or connect with me on social media. Contact me so that together we can do a Sales Strategy Audit on your business. In no time I can spot the gaps and see the opportunities to turn things around. If you are interested in finding out what working together would look like to accelerate your results, make a move. Dial the phone, tap out an e-mail, or send up a flare.

I hope that my words have touched, motivated, and inspired you to take some instantaneous and intentional action. Thank you for investing your time and allowing me to share what I was put on this planet to do.

May your life be blessed, your ideas become actions, your thoughts stay positive, your future be bright, and your business be filled with abundance.

www.lizwendling.com

303-929-3886

Don't Forget To Grab Your Free Audio: Evolved Selling Download: https://www.lizwendling.com/free-gift/

About The Author

Liz Wendling is a Sales Expert, Business Development Coach, Speaker, and Author, who works with clients around the country and internationally. She is an avid golfer and spends much of her free time in the majestic Colorado mountains.

Liz believes that everyone sells something, themselves, their ideas, or their products or services.

Liz helps companies and individuals revise and revamp their sales process, sales language, and sales approach, all of which create a profound difference in the way that they sell and communicate with their potential clients. Her services are in demand by those who are tired of following the masses and who want to break away from the pack and modernize their approach. She works with professionals who are eager to discover their own fresh signature selling style that fits them like a glove.

Whether it is next week, next month, or next year, connect with Liz about a specific tool, strategy, or idea that you ran with that made your sales and client conversion a breeze. And, of course, you get all the credit because you took the leap from idea to action, and action produces results!

In Liz's private coaching and training programs, she has assisted thousands of individuals with turning their business around and building the life that they wanted.

You are an e-mail or a phone call away from Liz. She is here to help you dash from mediocrity to fame and fortune! Discuss with her the program that works best for you. Please feel free to e-mail Liz at liz@lizwendling.com or call her at 303-929-3886.

If you are looking for a speaker for your next conference, sales meeting, or convention, hire Liz to share the power of selling with rock-solid sales confidence with your audience. She can deliver keynote, half-day, and full-day messages depending on your needs. To find out more, please visit www.lizwendling.com.

Made in the USA
Middletown, DE
16 January 2021